Endorsements for **Coming To Life:**

"Todd is one of the voices of our generation calling us to remember who we are; not just for our own sake, but for the sake of the generations to come! His voice is authentic and passionate, and has helped me awaken to my calling as one of the sons of the Father!"
Brian Doerksen, Songwriter, producer, recording artist and pastor

"Who are you?" is a profound question, and Todd Rutkowski shows us how profound it is in his Journey to Identity. This work is not a Bible study, but a profound biblical meditation in which biblical motifs are interwoven with impactful observations of human life."
Peter H. Davids, Ph.D., Professor, Houston Baptist University

"In this book Todd has creatively woven an inviting tapestry of stories, both personal and biblical, in order to draw us into the freedom of real community with God, ourselves and others. Writing out of his own experience, often with a disarming transparency, he effectively establishes some helpful signposts for those who dare to pursue such a journey of the heart."
Gary Best, National Director, Vineyard Churches Canada

"A Home Run! Todd truly reveals himself in this creative exposition, and in so doing, reveals each one of us. Experience the passion and the greater purpose for which this work has been created... for your identity, your passion and God's purpose for your life."
Frank Fabiano, Psychologist, Co-Founder of Dunamis Ministries and Co-Author of "Healing the Past, Releasing Your Future"

"At a time when much ecclesial strategy remains seeker focused in order to gain new adherents, Rutkowski envisions a broader proposal-the effective replicating of leadership for the next generation. Rutkowski offers a cogent contribution towards spiritual parenting in the church, with flair and conviction."
Dr. Paul Edward Hughes, Associate Professor of Religious Studies, Trinity Western University

"Todd's commitment to the next generation and to community has not wavered. While his vision has evolved, his call to discovering identity, passion and purpose in the place of community is tried and true."
David Ruis, Songwriter, worship leader, producer and church planter, Los Angeles, California

"Growing up with Todd has allowed me to see him live out what he writes not just as a brother but as a witness. I've watched him struggle, grow and find his place and voice. Not only is it an honour to call him my brother, it is a privilege to call him my friend."
Dean Rutkowski (Brother), Calgary, Alberta.

Cover Artwork by Boundless Interactive Media

ISBN 0-9712311-9-2

Published by VMI Publishers
Sisters, Oregon I P.O. Box 1676

Printed in the United States of America

Coming
to Life

The Journey to Identity, Passion and Purpose

Todd Michael Rutkowski

VMI Publishers
Sisters, Oregon

To my wife Maryanne –
You are the wind beneath my wings
To my four children Megan, Keelan, Jayden and Brianna–
I love you
To my brother, sister and mother–
We have journeyed together and have grown through pain
To my father who is no longer here with us–
Some things I will never know and some things will never make sense but you gave up your life and I now recognize the depth of your desperation and accept your choice.

TABLE OF CONTENTS

TO MY SPIRITUAL FATHERS

I dedicate this work to my many spiritual fathers, both men and women, who have imparted to me from God's heart along the way. Uncle Blaine, you were there for me when I needed someone as a young teenager. Uncle Gary, you called me out and made room for my fledgling passions. Uncle Murray, you taught me how to laugh and how not to take myself too seriously. Bernie and Bernice Doan, you treated me like a son and gave me a model of integrity to follow. Your words of approval have stayed in my heart. Bob Holland, you awakened me to God's call on my life, pointing to His purposes for my life. Marianne Sitton, you called out my hunger and thirst for God. Fubara Ibama, my African father, you gave me passion for God like no other. Frank Dorst, you showed me the way of grace, reminding me that the love of God often leaks out of us. Uli and Carol Kortsch, you cut a swath for me, allowing me to experience the fulfillment of many dreams. Dale Kauffman, you modeled transparency in leadership to me. You introduced me to the nations of the world and taught me how to dream, for which I am ever grateful. Frank and Catherine Fabiano, you were insightful, skilled instruments of healing to me. God used you to touch my clay. Paul Hawkins, you called out the educator within me, rounding off my purpose. David Boyd, you modeled to me the way of honesty and integrity in leadership. You gave me vision for relationships in leadership. Ross Colello, you believed in my dreams much more than I; you have given me wings to soar. Your godly response to unjust pain has taught me that God's favor is unshakeable. Mac and Louise Jardine, you gave me a renewed perspective on the work of the Holy Spirit and showed me God's love for the poor. Gary Best, you are the most complete leader I have encountered. Your color has rubbed off on me. You prepared me to be a spiritual father and a son. Each of you has been part of my community, passing on identity, passion, and purpose to me, and I am honored to be a part of your legacy.

Thank you for being my community.

CHAPTER 1
PASSING ON IDENTITY, PASSION AND PURPOSE

DISCOVERING THE ANCIENT PATH

"Let each generation tell its children of your mighty acts. I will meditate on your majestic, glorious splendor and your wonderful miracles."[1]

The morning sun pierced the horizon of the Congo basin with anticipation in its entrance, as if it, too, waited to mark that special day. Joined by the sun, the Congolese people began their yearly celebrations, which involved deep traditions that would mark the days' events. Morning often comes early for the families of this remote village along the Congo River northeast of Kinshasa. Yet this morning seemed to come even earlier, especially to the families whose boys were reaching manhood.

The celebrations passed down by their forefathers required that each boy who had turned thirteen in that year to participate in a series of rituals to prepare him for manhood. Every adult male in the village had taken this journey, which seemed to mark him forever in some mysterious way. With stories of those who had gone before them, the boys of the Okapi village embraced this day with both excitement and terror at the chance to earn their manhood.

Flanked by his elders, a rather sullen and aloof chief became purposeful and engaged on this special day. It was as though he knew what this meant to his people, to these boys and to their future. One could tell by the significance he placed on his involvement and the involvement of the rest of the village that it was more than a duty-filled ritual. It was a living and dynamic reality teeming with passion and purpose, bringing life again to the chief and to the young men to be.

The Chief invited the boys into his sacred lodge, which only the men of the tribe and the elders entered, the first indicator of the value placed on this moment. In the most peaceful yet vulnerable language and demeanor, the chief began to call these young boys to something greater than themselves: manhood. He spoke to them about their people and invited them to take their place in the community for its greater good. He spoke of their need of them as a village and his underlying assurance that he was pleased with each one of them, even before they faced the challenges of the days to come. He told them stories of their collective past: times of plenty and of times of want. He told them of wars won and lost, of heroes and villains. He defined the symbols that marked their unique story as a people. Finally, he prepared them for what they would face in the coming days.

This "rite of passage" every boy must face to become a man was theirs for the taking; it was now within their reach. He told them whom they would meet in the jungle: themselves. He called each one to face himself, his fears, and the overwhelming aloneness that would strike when least expected. He fully knew they would return as men and gave them that assurance. With a brief smile and a glimmer of hope in his eyes, he motioned them away from his presence, knowing what they yet did not know.

The young boys were then met by the women of the village and given the ceremonial preparation for death - death of childhood.[2] Each boy was carefully separated from the others and bathed in an earthy pigment that was a blend of roots, jungle leaves and clay. This ritual symbolized the elements of life being put to death, as a new element of life would emerge from this death. The final ritual began with the random placement of markings across the body, identifying characteristics of each one's childhood.

The capstone of this ritual was a tearful one, as each mother carefully painted the face of her own son in blue - the symbol of death. With the markings of the "death of childhood" evident to all, each boy found his way through the village to be met by the elders at the jungle's edge. Filled with mixed emotions, each villager turned away from the boys, as one must not look at the face of death. The feelings of separation and aloneness were often unearthed by these events setting the emotional stage for its climactic finish.

Each boy has heard the story of another, yet each boy must write his own story now; he cannot live through another man's life. Each boy was escorted to a remote location in the jungle where he would be left to fend for himself, not returning without the tail of a boar in hand. For some boys it meant days, for others weeks, yet for all it seemed a lifetime.

It is the first evening of the first day and all seemed familiar, which removed the edge off their emotions for at least a moment. The sounds of jungle were recognizable: the rushing water, the crow of the Toucan, the faint brushing of the elephant off in the distance. The smells brought back memories of hunting with the men of the village - the leaves, the flowers and the poisonous berries. As night fell that first evening the familiar jungle became a foreign place. Having never slept in the jungle, the boys were unprepared for the transformation the jungle experienced as darkness appeared. The memory of the words of the village men rushed through their minds telling them the jungle floor was no place to find refuge at night. Finding sanctuary in the branches of a tree was short-lived, as every unfamiliar sound proved to make for a long and sleepless first night.

The morning sun appeared to delay its arrival that second day. Awakened by hunger the boys slithered down from their chair- like beds and began that day's hunt for food. The growing hunger pains proved a great asset to eventually solving the problem. Hunger, an amazing tool to engage the memory, motivated action. They spent most of the second day, hungry and confused, attempting to pull from their memory snapshots of the village men finding food in the jungle. With each passing hour, hunger gave way to determination and determination gave way to resolve. Some discovered the satisfaction of the bland plant life while others mastered the art of hunting prey - meals without fire, of course. Fire would be another day's accomplishment.

As darkness fell on the second day each boy found comfort in the fact that he had made it through the day and found hope in the reality that he made it through the previous night. The second night was met with less anxiety, although innovation had not yet taken a role in determining where and how to sleep. Something was building inside each boy, something subtle and yet profound. Simple things had meaning now. By the third and fourth night something more than familiarity was setting in. Something far more profound was happening. Amidst the fear and hunger, identity and purpose were being formed in them. Each boy was becoming a man. They recognized that on the other side of fear was hope, if they would just find the courage to face it. They also discovered new things about themselves, having no one to fill the gap and take up the slack. They were learning a little bit more about who they were, which often does not reveal itself until it is forced out into the open. Each day built one more layer of manhood at a great risk, of course, the risk that they would retreat back into childhood ways.

With their senses acute and their focus growing one by

one and at different times in the journey, each boy broke through the barrier of childhood and could now hunt as a young man. One by one the memories of the hunt for the cherished boar came back to them. There were times when they were present in the hunt as a child, yet without retaining the knowledge for such a time as this. They were simply and innocently experiencing the thrill of the chase. That time was over and they must find the skills to complete the task as young men.

Some found the boar first, while others remembered the strategy of the chase first. Either way, each one eventually cornered their boar. With the end in sight each boy unknowingly was finding identity, passion and purpose starting to take root in his heart. They had earned the right to be men. With the tail of the boar in hand, the sense of accomplishment was indescribable that day. The blue pigment now washed from each face, they returned to the waiting village to be embraced as young men. A celebration involving the preparation of the whole village took place as the culmination of this rite of passage.

"They know when childhood ends, when adulthood begins and what their society expects of them."[3] Everything was designed towards this message, this focus and this outcome - "You belong, you are needed and there is a place for you in this world." Identity, passion and purpose had been awakened in each boy through this experience only to be satisfied through an ever-increasing awareness of that reality.

PRIMITIVE OR BIBLICAL

In the Western World we stand back from this story with its rich cultural markings unaware of its impact on the next generation. Having little context for a story such as this, we who live in the West see it through our rugged, individualistic colored glasses, making us even less aware of what we lose in the profound reality defined in this so-called primitive culture. For many of us in the Western World we would brand this experience primitive. We may, however, find it intriguing, or we may become attracted by its antiquity in a world where things seem disposable, especially traditions. Yet there is something profound, something visionary and brilliant, at work here that Western Civilization could overlook, if we choose to look at it without taking off our colored glasses. Otherwise we would try to understand such an experience without understanding its context.

No culture could be defined as God's culture. Every culture has elements that speak of the character of God and his Kingdom, and elements that take us away from that very reality. Discerning those elements can be a lifelong process in discovering the character of God through His Word called the Holy Scriptures.

It was however, the Hebrew culture that formed the womb into which God planted the seed that He nurtured for thousands of years for His plan of world redemption. It was to that culture that He entrusted the formation and the passing on of the Old Testament, part of the Holy Scriptures, from one generation to the next. God defined Himself at times by their culture's role models, giving us a model for how identity and purpose are formed and discovered. Therefore, the culture of the Old Testament gives us some common ground from which to measure our story from the Congo basin.

This culture in the remote Congo understood a very basic biblical framework about the relationship and roles of one generation to another. In the book of Exodus, God first declares Himself to Moses as the God of Abraham, Isaac and Jacob. God did not just identify Himself as the God of Abraham but identified Himself by three generations as though they are interconnected. Both God and later Abraham realized that identity, passion and purpose are formed over generations. Our lives are built upon one another, resulting in both the responsibility and the privilege of passing on this identity, passion, and purpose so that the next generation can build on it. The Bible itself, though written as sixty-six independent books, is not just a book of independent short stories. Although written at different times by different people from different perspectives, it is one interconnected story from start to finish. Woven together through people, races and cultures, it is a work of genius that was authored by God and reflects His character.

In Psalm 78 in verses 1-7 the Psalmist Asaph writes, *"O my people listen to my teaching, open your ears to what I am saying, for I will speak to you in a parable. I will teach you hidden lessons from our past- stories we have heard and know, stories our ancestors handed down to us. We will not hide these truths from our children but will tell the next generation about the glorious deeds of the Lord. We will tell of his mighty power and the mighty miracles he did. For he issued a decree to Jacob; he gave his law to Israel. He commanded our ancestors to teach them to their children, so the next generation might know them - even the children not yet born - that they in turn might teach their children. So each generation can set its hope anew on God, remembering his glorious miracles and obeying his commands."[4]*

The call of the Old Testament and the Hebrew culture was to pass on from one generation to the next the things of God. It was the call to see life as bigger than our own lives.

DEFINING A LEGACY

Many Western Christians have not made the connection in how life is defined and ultimately measured. Our lives have bookends, limiting our ability to capture reality. We believe our impact is measured by what happens from the day we are born until the day our name appears on a tombstone. Some people may even be passionate about following God and want to give their whole lives to him, and many do, but at the expense of and without thought to the next generation - both their spiritual and biological children.

Our life is not all we have to offer God, although it is where we must start. Nor is our life just measured by the bookends of our birth and death. We do not see as God sees in this matter. In our tunnel vision we miss the interconnected purposes of God. As Edward Sellner said, "Each of us contains within our fragile vessels of skin and bones and cells this inheritance of soul. We are links between the ages, containing past and present expectations, sacred memories, and future promise. Only when we recognize that we are heirs can we truly be pioneers."[5]

Abraham's legacy was dependent on the quality of those he left behind to fulfill a three-generational calling. Abraham's legacy and call was dependent on his next generation's obedience and could not be defined without them. His life was defined by faith; the bookends of his birth and death would have been far too narrow to define his legacy. It took time to put this in perspective and to see its full impact. The future was out of his control, but not beyond his influence. The seed was miraculously given to Abraham; the seed was then established in Isaac, his son, and the seed was named and multiplied in Jacob, his grandson. For this reason God defines them by one another and defines himself by all three: *the God of Abraham, Isaac and Jacob*.

I recall at the end of my fourth year of college, while living in the United States, the opportunity to return to Canada. I was invited by a fellow student to move to Northern Alberta to look for work on the oil rigs with the hopes of making quick money. What excited me most about the idea was that I would be close to my grandfather, Oliver Lefebvre, my mother's father, and I had wanted to be near him for sometime.

I arrived in Cold Lake, Alberta at my grandfather's home, to his delight. While I only lived up in the north for four months, during that time he and I had quality time together. I sat with him in his living room on a few occasions, asking every question that came to mind. Tell me about your childhood, Grandpa; tell me about your life, your mistakes, your hopes, and your dreams. He loved to talk and I really wanted to listen.

There was a deep bond that occurred between my grandfather and me during that time. As the oldest grandchild of twenty grandchildren I felt privileged to be hearing the things of his heart because I knew he would not be around forever. I recall him telling me of the many dramatic answers to his prayers and of his relationship with God. My grandfather was a simple man but had a deep faith that I had not known before. I left those months feeling enriched by his life.

The relationship cultivated in that season came out of an invitation I had from him several years earlier. His brother-in-law was dying of cancer when I was sixteen years old. Along with his son Murray, my uncle, the two of them felt that representatives of three generations should be present to pray for healing for Uncle Arthur. I was invited to be that third generation. As I prepared for that time, excited to pray for healing, indirectly I would receive from my grandfather the passing on of a legacy that neither he nor I had anticipated. Uncle Arthur did not get healed of cancer and died shortly after, but that did not seem to affect my faith. I still continue to pray for healing and since then I have seen many healed.

However, what did occur is a deposit from one generation to another. My grandfather was unknowingly imparting something to me about who I was and my future. He validated me and invited me to relationship and to what he deemed as important work.

When my grandfather eventually died on December 11th, 1995, I was amazed at the impact on me emotionally. I felt naked and uncovered for quite a long period of time. When I was asked to give the eulogy at his funeral, though aware of his humanity and shortcomings, it was not those that mattered most to me or would define his life for me. Rather it was the deposit into my life and the lives of others that became apparent. I realized who I am today has much to do with his life and his prayers for me. My grandfather's legacy lives on through my life simply because he took time to tell me and invite me into meaningful experiences with him.

Our lives are measured and defined primarily by succession, by how we spiritually prepare and invest in those coming along behind us and beside us. The naturally sullen and aloof chief of a primitive tribe came alive during the rite of passage ritual; because he knew that his investing in the next generation's identity, passion and purpose was ultimately defining his own existence.

Drawing on the past, we stand in the present and speak into the future. It is the future that gives meaning to the past. This perspective should greatly impact how we live life. When we define life by our direct impact we either evaluate it inaccurately or we hold on to it too long, missing the opportunity of greater value having given things away at the right time. This narrow vision of reality keeps us in fear, while keeping our future generations floundering in their identity, their God-given passions and their undiscovered purpose.

THE POWER TO INVEST

Picture the story of the Exodus of the nation of Israel out of their captivity in Egypt as a movie set. Envision God as the director of this movie. During the shooting of a powerful and dramatic scene, the director interrupts the set to ask the cast a riveting question: "How are you going to pass this experience on to the next generation- as you must?" God yells, "Cut!" to talk to the lead character, Joshua. In the story, God is about to cut off the waters of Jordan so His people can cross on dry land to reach the destiny promised to them and their forefathers.[6]

In this moment, the director (God) talks to the lead character, Joshua. He speaks to Joshua about gathering twelve leaders, one from each tribe, in order to mark this dramatic event. A memorial made of stones was to be placed at the river's edge so the story could be passed on to the next generation. God was inviting each member of that community to invest in the next generation and the memorial made it possible

God was standing with them in the present, reaching into the past and inviting them to speak into the future. God stepped in as a father, helping them find a means for wide participation in telling the story. God invited Joshua to open the door so that everyone could be involved in the passing of identity to those who would follow behind them. Making the story memorable and accessible, everyone could participate. As each generation looked at the memorial stones piled on the Jordan's banks, they could retell the story of who they were and who God was to them.

After graduating from junior college in 1954 John Wimber[7] became an accomplished musician. "In 1962 he bought an up-and-coming musical group called the Righteous Brothers and played sax for them. In 1964 they released their hit single, "You've Lost that Lovin' Feeling" and were booked to support the Beatles at the start of their American tour in San Francisco,"[8] when God encountered John and changed his life direction.

Little did he know how much his life would shape a significant part of the evangelical church in the latter part of the twentieth century. His introduction to the evangelical practices of Christianity was filled with confusion. He often wondered when they got to *"do the stuff"* as he called it. When did they get to attempt the things Jesus did, like pray for the sick, cast out demons and care for the poor that he read in the Scriptures? That struggle formed the foundation of John Wimber's contribution. He provided an *"on ramp"* for the more conservative Evangelicals to participate in the ministry of Jesus. He took participation with the work of the Holy Spirit in healing and setting the oppressed free and placed it completely in the hands of every Christian. As a result, he took it out of the hands of a few professionals or *"anointed ones"* and put it back into the hands of the Church.

While Wimber was not the first or the last to visit this issue, his leadership challenged, called, and equipped thousands of Christians in the latter part of the twentieth century to participate in the ministry of Jesus again. The previous specialization that had existed in a large portion of the evangelical church, though safer, had minimized the effectiveness and the breadth of the ministry Jesus had come to leave with his Church. Like Joshua, God seemed to invite John Wimber to open wide the door of participation in telling and living the story.

Prior to Wimber and the influence of a few others like him, the broader population of evangelical leadership, in a rather opposite manner, had continued to place their investment into the next generation in the hands of a few trusted professionals, erecting a barricade against the wider participation of the community. As a result, this specialization widened the gap between generations and robbed the community of God from having the privilege of investing into the identity, passions and purpose of their succeeding generation. Like the Congolese Chief and his elders, we should be able to see the future in our next generation and invest in them now as a whole community or village.

Without a community that crosses class, race, and generations, the link to sustainable life is weakened. The immature mentor the less mature, and the apparent lack of diverse relationship creates an unhealthy and barren homogenization of community. It is the power of the diverse members of a community that allows identity, passion and purpose to be passed on and formed within us, not just a few specialized professionals.

If I am connected to the first community (God), no personal threat to my existence is created. I can be rejected or injured, but I cannot be destroyed. So with that assurance I can enter community with human beings. As we open the door for many to participate in passing on identity, passion and purpose we open the door for connection. Without connection we have no community and without community we fall short on discovery.

According to Larry Crabb, "connecting is at the center of [community]".[9] It is our capacity to connect as humans that gives meaning to our distinctiveness among living things. The rugged individualism and chosen isolation of our western culture violates the very nature of our humanity, the need to connect, forcing us to live outside of our true nature.

The genesis for our connection is with God. God is a connected community - Father, Son and Holy Spirit. God is the first community and connecting to him is where life begins. Disconnection from God as the foremost community can mean that the most intimate part of us is connected to no one, declaring us unknown. Larry Crabb indicates that this disconnection drives us "to exchange superior longings for lesser ones, allowing us to settle for success and concentrated but shallow relationships rather than connection."[10]

When that first community resides inside us as followers of Christ, then connection can occur one to another. Connection, the center of community, occurs, as Larry Crabb would say "when the life of Christ in me touches the life of Christ in you."[11]

To enter into community requires more of me than being physically present. It requires vulnerability, transparency and humility. To fully enter into our identity, passion and purpose requires community. The road to discovery for the individual requires the whole. No one can find oneself alone. No one can be fully known outside community. I must know that to enter community through the gateway of vulnerability, transparency and honesty, it cannot destroy me, or I cannot readily enter.

In reality, we need trained and capable workers in the community; we would be lost without them. Yet we should not underestimate how much our next generation needs us, as ordinary people connected to God, to connect to them. We need to take the spiritual future of our nations into our own hands as we take our financial futures into our own hands. If we see the next generation like spiritual savings plans we may understand the importance of making small deposits now and thinking about their impact. The future benefit of an IRA or RSP investment is dependent on the investments we make today. The little deposits today can reap large dividends over time. Our next generation, like our financial future, demands that we all personally invest to share in the benefits. Our investment is in our connection.

THE CALL TO SPIRITUAL FATHERING

Our children are living messages we send to a time and place we will never see."[12]

The call to us is to spiritually father our next generation. Either we learn how to father them or we stand by as others do it for us. The question is not: "Will they be fathered?" rather, the question is: "By whom will they be fathered?" The primary responsibility of a father is to tell his children who they are and where they belong, while giving them a context in which to discover their purpose. Spiritual fathering is not a gender issue. God is father and it is His role to father His children. Yet He does this through people, through men or through women. God, taking His place as Father, desires to build identity, passion and purpose into the lives of the next generation of young men and women. Yet it is those connected to Him that He authorizes to tell this next generation His heart for them.

Herein lies the problem for us today in the Western World. Many people born since the early 1960s have not received fathering of this nature themselves. They are struggling for identity. Men struggle to find their "rite of passage" experience into manhood, and women give themselves away emotionally in relationships before they know their own identity. It is neglect that makes even that generation aware of the need, mysteriously heightening the value and recognition of spiritual fathering.

Joseph, the son of Jacob, written about in the Old Testament was abandoned by his siblings and cut off from fathering. He was taken to prison, neglected and banished from purpose and meaning. Joseph, after being released from prison, was placed in a high-ranking position in Egypt. During a famine that affected his estranged family, he had the opportunity to give back to his siblings and father what he had not been given. Neglect does not disqualify one from spiritually fathering; only lack of vision or choosing not to receive God's fathering can restrain us.

Michael was born in Poland in 1887. For many years he and his family carved out a living in the eastern part of Poland or what was then the Ukraine. He became an accomplished blacksmith. There was no preparation, however, for the raw and unpredictable events to follow in Michael's life. Germany had declared War on Russia in August of 1914, beginning its rise to power. Poland became a target of Germany and was the first of many countries to experience this nation's and its' Allies' wrath. During that time, with the events and details uncertain, Michael along with his brother Jake discovered their relatives executed with no forewarning. The two men were the only ones kept alive and were marched off to a remote and distant prison.

For several years they remained in captivity, all the while preparing an escape. With the slaying of two guards on their hands, they fought their way to freedom, only to realize it was too painful and too perilous to return to Poland during the 1930s. Finding transportation through Europe and then across the Atlantic Ocean to Canada is where the instinct to survive took them.

Eventually finding his way to the Canadian Province of Saskatchewan, Michael, now in his fifties, began a family. As his oldest adopted son, along with his three biological boys, began to grow up, the pain of his unresolved past could not remain unvisited. His aging mind and body could not contain the pain of his past. Drinking started to take over his life. His alcohol abuses led to bouts of anger and fury resulting in his four sons distancing themselves from him.

Michael's second son, Wally, found the pain and the poverty too great to bear. Desperate to protect his heart, at seventeen years of age, he deserted his father and mother for the city, hoping to make something of himself. With intellect and genius to lead him, he quickly found his way into the work force, excelling at everything he touched, especially computers.

Emerging as a top computer analyst in just a few short years, the world began making a place for him. He was in full stride with success in hand and a young family at his side when his unresolved past began to appear.

Like his father, he, too, turned to alcohol to conceal his painful past. Believing he had his drinking under control, he carried on his life with flare for several more years. Anchored in the illusion that he had the world by the tail, he did not anticipate the influence his unresolved past was yet to play in his life. With a growing instability and hidden binges of drunkenness, his personal life began to slowly unravel while his professional life mysteriously blossomed. His great intellect and charismatic personality, which made him a person of promise, was now his greatest stumbling block. It was his intellect that kept him from believing in spiritual reality and his charisma that kept him alone in his misery. Instead of reaching to others and to God, the only One Who could father him, he reached for himself. In this desperate period, God interrupted his life, giving him supernatural dreams and experiences but they brought no relief from the torment in his life, as he did not fully embrace them.

Eventually his professional and personal worlds completely unraveled and his family left him for their own safety. During that time, he cried out to God. It was then that he experienced peace for the first time in his spirit. Though he walked out his spiritual journey with a greater sense of personal peace and relief at times over the following year he could not sustain freedom from his addictions. His family, which had reunited with him a year later, soon departed for the second and final time.

In the final moments of Wally's life, at age thirty-nine, he telephoned his children to tell each of them that he loved them deeply. He then spoke over the phone to his wife, telling her that he could not win the battle over his addictions and that he must take himself out for their sake. When I, the first born of those children, heard him tell me that he loved me and then three days later received the news of his death, I was undone. At fifteen I had lost my father and now needed to face the issue of abandonment. I, too, became faced with how I would choose to be fathered and how I would choose to face my pain. The cycle could continue or be broken. A promise from God to me pierced my heart during those traumatic days from the Holy Scriptures - Psalm 27:10. *"Even if my father and mother abandon me, the Lord will hold me close."* (NLT) That promise is the story of my life and the story I now write about, that God can father the fatherless if we will just allow him to touch us directly and touch us through community.

As a child of alcoholism and a son who was cut off early from fathering, by the premature death of my earthly father, I, too, come to this table called spiritual fathering with a partially empty plate. Yet I come with great vision and great hope knowing that God will father the fatherless through anyone daring enough to enter into his heart for another.

Spiritual fathering is how one generation passes identity, passion and purpose to the next one. Spiritual fathering is what the people of Israel did under Joshua, what Abraham, Isaac and Jacob defined and what the Congolese chief and his village participated in together. They all saw God's purposes established beyond their lifetime and their legacy and meaning was found in those who came after them.

Chapter 1
Process Questions

1. What experiences in your life have contributed to your "rite of passage" to adulthood?

2. How have you invested in those coming behind?

3. What have you received from those who have gone before? (affirmation, resources, provision, blessing)

4. If spiritual fathering is telling someone who they are, where they belong and giving them a place to discover their purpose, how would you then describe how you have been fathered?

5. On a scale of 1-10 (1 being low and 10 being high) how effectively are you spiritually fathering others?

6. What is the number one roadblock to you spiritually fathering others?

CHAPTER 2
WAITING TO BE FOUND

HIDE AND SEEK

The nature of spiritual community provides the capacity and components to recognize and support the discovery of identity. When a community is involved in the process of discovery, identity is more likely to be secured, especially in the lives of the next generation. We may remember that moment in the childhood game of hide and seek, sitting in the dark, tucked away in some hiding spot, wondering if we would ever be found, only to discover that the game had ended and the other kids had forgotten we were still hiding. We love to play hide and seek as kids because we love to hide and we love to be found. I watched my own children play this game with their neighborhood friends.

Watching the game through my adult eyes made obvious their desire to be seen, giving away the fact that they longed to be found. A simple but universal longing is touched in this childhood experience. There is a part of us that enjoys the dark and likes to think we can fool others, yet there is a whole other part of us that is deeply offended if we are not found.

Sometimes in life we actually hide so we can be found and sometimes in our hiding we are not found. We all need to know that someone acknowledges and values our presence; someone cares if we are not present and that someone will look for us until we are found. This longing, though a universal one, has a spiritual nature to it. It is a longing deposited there by our Father in heaven, and it is only He who can find us completely. At the heart of our disconnection with God is fatherlessness and homelessness.

At the heart of fatherlessness and homelessness is the question of belonging. When we recognize that this longing can compel us to climb the tallest of mountains, to champion the biggest of causes or to throw our lives away to passiveness, bitterness or self-destruction, we become genuinely humbled. We are humbled because we recognize our deep vulnerability to doubt His love and search for ourselves, because we do not yet believe anyone is seriously looking for us. Because it is God's love we doubt, our search for belonging, outside of Him, becomes futile. The vulnerability I speak of was touched in the story of a young man who desperately needed to be found just like we do. In a most unorthodox way, he was playing hide and seek.

IDENTITY LOST AND FOUND

"Now a man named Lazarus was sick. He was from Bethany, the village of Mary and her sister Martha. This Mary, whose brother Lazarus now lay sick, was the same one who poured perfume on the Lord and wiped his feet with her hair. So the sisters sent word to Jesus, Lord, the one you love is sick.... Jesus loved Martha and her sister and Lazarus. Yet when he heard that Lazarus was sick, he stayed where he was two more days.... On his arrival, Jesus found that Lazarus had already been in the tomb for four days.... When Mary reached the place where Jesus was and saw him, she fell at his feet and said, "Lord, if you had been here, my brother would not have died." When Jesus saw her weeping, and the Jews who had come along with her also weeping, he was deeply moved in spirit and troubled. "Where have you laid him?" He asked. "Come and see Lord," they replied. Jesus wept. The Jews said, "See how he loved him." But some said, "Could not He who opened the eyes of the blind man, have kept this man from dying?" [13]

Lazarus was faced with the question of his belonging

and his identity at the most vulnerable moment of his life. At a time when he could not find himself or save himself he cried out to the one who he believed loved him—Jesus. On his death bed I am sure his sisters assured him that they had told Jesus of his condition, all of them completely anticipating he would respond. They told Jesus that Lazarus was waiting to be found – "the one you love is sick"[14]. Yet Jesus did not respond immediately. He left Lazarus in his misery and pain, alone and uncomforted. Lazarus was left waiting by the only One who could truly find him completely. This waiting may have cut deep into his heart, discharging a reservation about his love. I can only imagine the kinds of thoughts that haunted his deteriorating state of mind, potentially unearthing the security of love he thought he knew. *Why isn't Jesus coming? I thought he loved me. I thought he would come and find me and let me know I belong to him.*

The security of Jesus' love had weathered the storm until now, but its waning was demonstrated in Martha's outspoken doubt, which now held ransom her security in his love. She had said, "If you had been here, my brother would not have died"[15].

In the life of Lazarus we see the vulnerability of our identity and our need to know God loves us. What we know from Lazarus' life is death does not have the final say. It is not the defining issue for securing doubt in us nor does it have the final vote— God does. Like the childhood game of hide and seek, I am sure Lazarus and his sisters thought the game was over and he was still left unfound. Yet every adult and every young person must cross the threshold of having their belonging and identity tested. Everyone in pursuit of identity must come to the river's edge of doubt and look across it, knowing they must wade through it, silently hoping they will not be swept away by its current. It is in knowing this, that we are completely and fully loved by

God, where our identity must ultimately come to rest if we are ever to be secure.

LAZARUS AND THE NEED TO BE LOVED

Many of us and many of the lives of our next generation resemble the life of Lazarus. They are lives lived in doubting God's love. They are lives where circumstances have unearthed the question of belonging and love, leaving identity sliding through our grasp.

For example, the profile of our generation born on the eve of the new millennium has reason to doubt His love. It is a profile of misery and pain, where they have been left alone and uncomforted, like Lazarus. One in two families will end up in divorce and "one in five children do not have a father in their life on a regular basis and equitable basis."[16] Violence and abuse are out of control, fatherlessness is an epidemic and drug use is widespread. Abandonment and neglect define many lives.

The ones Jesus loves are sick. The ones that are waiting to be found are dying while doubting his love. He is moved with compassion and moved towards us and them, as he was Lazarus. He is aware that we doubt His love, and He is alert to the reality that we often feel He is too late.

He waited until Lazarus was dead for four days. He waited until Lazarus and his sisters thought the game of hide and seek was over and that Lazarus had been left, only to be forgotten. Yet it is into this kind of hopelessness that Jesus brought identity and belonging. Lazarus was the one He loves and that is who we are: the one He loves. In the story of one person, Lazarus, we experience the truth of the universal love of God expressed to human beings, while we identify with our own human propensity to doubt His love.

In her book Walking on Water: Reflections on Faith and Art, Madeleine L'Engle says, "When I was a child my parents loved me not because I was good, but because I was their child. I loved them, and I wanted to please them, but their love of me did not have to be earned. Neither does the love of God. We are loved because we are His children, because *we are*."[17] When the circumstances of our life have unearthed our doubt about His love we, like Lazarus, are invited to come to the place where we are secure in His love just because *we are*.

IDENTITY IS LINKED TO KNOWING YOUR NAME

Telling others who they are involves many things, but it starts with one thing - naming them. *"Our identity is linked to knowing our name"*, my friend Joyce Satter often declared to me. It is true that our name is more than just the letters that make up a word by which people refer to us. Our name defines us and our life defines our name. Madeleine L'Engle's says, "But we, the creatures, are named, and our names are part of our wholeness." [18] We are named by what we do and what we do not do throughout our formative years. We are named by our hobbies or by the type of people with whom we associate. We are named by our appearance, race and sexuality. The time in history and the generation with which we most identify influences our name. We may have many names and many people may name us, forming who we become rather than necessarily describing who we are.

Naming is the gift one generation is to give to another. It was the privilege of Abraham to name Isaac and Isaac, Jacob. L'Engle says, "God asked Adam to name all the animals, which was asking Adam to help in the creation of their wholeness. When we name each other, we are sharing in the joy and privilege of incarnation."[19]

Naming in its most primitive form is telling someone who they are and how God sees them. It is telling them first of all they are the one He loves. "To name is to love. To be named is to be loved,"[20] says L'Engle. If we do not understand the gravity of forming identity in our next generation, which comes in naming, then we leave a generation vulnerable to doubt His love, vulnerable to be named by anyone. Often what we name people are who they become, knowingly or unknowingly. If the members of the community do not participate in naming, doubt will name them.

There are three reasons people long to have someone name them:

"It helps them understand aspects of themselves— especially what [they] do not know about [themselves]. [Secondly] it affirms what they already know in their heart when they realize someone else sees these qualities in them and [thirdly] it gives them the security to have someone tell them things about themselves which they may feel they have to hide from others."[21] When we know our name, having been affirmed by others in our community, we will not respond to another name. Naming is the privilege of telling someone the qualities that make him unique; it is prophecy demystified.

I decided to give my seven-year-old son a gift one day. That gift was the gift of starting to intentionally name him. I said, "Keelan come here for a minute, Daddy has a gift for you." His eyes widened and a grin appeared as he hurried to my presence. I said, "Sit down for a minute; I want to give you something."

"What, Dad, what is it?", he said.

I replied, "I want to tell you something about what I see in you." His body slumped. "Keelan, I have noticed that you are very creative; you have a natural ability to see things in different ways and come up with amazing ideas. I have noticed you are very sensitive and are the first to recognize when people are hurting, or their feelings are hurt. You really love people and that shows."

I continued on with a few more things and then sat back anticipating his response of gratefulness, only to hear, "Is that it? I thought you said you were going to give me a gift." I replied, "I did, and the gift was telling you some wonderful things about who you are."

Moments later he ran outside, returning to play. All the while I am thinking, *So much for that having any impact.* About a half hour later he came back to me, looked at me and said, "Megan does not think I am creative."

I smiled, realizing in his own childlike way he had received my gift into his heart and needed assurance it was true. You see, after he had left he went outside to share with his older sister what I had told him and it was met with doubt. Alfred H. Ells in his book "Family Love" says, "How many hopes and fears, how many ardent wishes and anxious apprehensions are twisted together in the threads that connect the parent with the child?"[22]

At Christmas a few years ago I decided to write all three of my children a letter that I would later read out loud to them during the school break. I wanted to describe and put to language the embryonic characteristics I saw emerging in them while expressing my complete acceptance to each of them in a language they could hear. I vividly remember the moment, all three sitting together, looking at me with hunger in their eyes, as though I was about to feed them a meal. Their hearts were drinking in life as I simply communicated my heart to them. The spirit of my words was being absorbed into their bodies as I felt them soaking up my thoughts. In that moment I realized the weight of my impact upon them. They needed me not just to think my thoughts about them but also to verbalize them and to tell them who they were.

Naming is not a one-time event; it is communication that is required over and over, in many ways and forms, by many voices, to secure our identity. If we do not tell those coming after us what we see in their lives and what God sees in their lives someone else will give them a different name. That name may define them and yet not be God's name for them.

FINDING PEACE IN YOUR DESIGN

Often we hear people say, or maybe we have said, "I don't like my nose, or I wish I had a different skin color. What if I had been tall like my father? If I had been born in another time in history or to a different family, my life would be better."

My daughter Megan, who we think has beautiful, full and in-vogue lips often, says to us, "I don't like my lips; they are too big."

There is something deep and unconscious within the brokenness of many of our lives that leaves us believing that there are flaws in our design. Somehow if the things we cannot change could be changed, life would be complete. Yet this longing is a reflection of our core struggle for belonging and acceptance. We are not convinced that we are completely and unconditionally embraced by our Creator. We don't really believe that we are unconditionally loved. If we could just change the design, we would be complete.

There is no question that our lives reflect aspects of our broken humanity and our lives ooze that brokenness each time we interact with another. However, it is not the brokenness of our lives that defines us, it is our design and to whom we belong. It is God Who defines our belonging and gives us that deep inner sense of home. We do not always hold onto that truth however; like a helium balloon we become filled and then slowly leak out the fullness of that truth, requiring a refilling.

Some of us have never found home, have never found

the One who loves us most and completely. Until we do, we will struggle with the unmovable characteristics of our lives. Who can determine where they would like to be born, either the richest or the poorest of places? Who has control over which family they are entrusted to on earth? When has anyone experienced time travel outside the movies, finding a home in another time in history? Who can alter their gender without altering their design? Who can will their size and shape, color and race? Who can stop their family from being their family? None of us can and none of us should try. They are the unchangeable aspects of our design that we must come to terms with and find peace. [23]

In the unfolding epic of *Forest Gump*, an intense moment involving Lieutenant Dan, a man struggling with his sudden sad and harsh reality, God comes to the forefront of the movie. Having just lost his legs in the Vietnam War, Lieutenant Dan's return to America was met with further loss—his dignity and place in society. His shattered reality disputed his core value. He eventually found his way to Forest Gump, a simple man and a former soldier under his command, who had only respect for him. Forest welcomed Lieutenant Dan into the life of *"shrimping"* with him.

One day while at work on a shrimp boat Lieutenant Dan found himself at sea caught in the eye of a storm. With gale force winds and torrents of rain engulfing him, Lieutenant Dan remained in the storm. It was in this moment that he chose not to flee the storm but instead to struggle with his Maker. The storm became the catalyst to connect Lieutenant Dan to his struggle with his Maker over his harsh existence. The scene ends with the storm dissipated and Lieutenant Dan having now settled things with his Maker is at peace with himself.

The sequence in the movie captures the raw struggle of man against God. The struggle and agony we must all face with our Creator, until we find peace with Him regarding our existence. Yet even when we do find it the first time, we must continually go back to that place of struggling with Him over our belonging and being loved. Like a helium balloon we seem to slowly leak out that which fills us and sustains us. We seem to be born with a penetrable spirit, which leaks out our sense of love and belonging from time to time. We lose our grasp on the reality of being completely loved again and again. As we look to our lives and the lives of our next generation we recognize that telling them who they are involves helping them come to terms with their design and serving them by pointing them to the core issue of belonging and being loved by being filled again and again with the truth. *"And I pray that Christ will be more and more at home in your hearts as you trust him. May your roots go down deep into the soil of God's marvellous love. And may you have the power to understand, as all God's people should, how wide, how long, how high and how deep his love really is. May you experience the love of Christ, though it is so great you will never fully understand it."*[24]

IDENTITY: WHO WE ARE, NOT WHAT WE DO

It was a most unusual October. We had just finished a satisfying venture, the gathering of over five thousand young people from more than one hundred and twenty five nations in Atlanta, Georgia. Our dream had been to bring the nations of the world together to worship God in their unique cultural expressions while meeting new friends, and giving the world a human face. We would then, as over a hundred different teams, spread out across the continent to inner cities and remote locations of comparable ethnic neighborhoods, to express God's love and kindness to those we would meet.

We chose to come along side the 1996 Olympics games being held in Atlanta, Georgia, as visas were much more accessible to certain nations during those times. Although it took four years of preparation and intense work, its impact would not be known for years to come, maybe never. Serving at that time for several years as the North American Director for the organization that hosted this gathering, I found myself satisfied, yet unsettled upon completion of the experience.

On one hand I was building and leading the vision I had dreamed of since college, yet on the other hand God was doing more work within me that I was yet to understand. Unsettled and unclear, I was given the option of leaving that place of privilege and success to join a church plant in my local area. Initially the idea did not connect with me, but when it caught my wife Maryanne's attention, I considered it further. It later impacted me when we both chose to take the month of October to pray and ask God His thoughts on it all.

I had just returned from forty-eight hours of being alone with my thoughts and with God. It took almost the entire time just to quiet myself and my hasty mind. How could I even consider walking away now? I had been at this for eight years and had a network of incredible relationships building around the world. Besides I was doing what I had set out to do—build an infrastructure for the next generation to follow God's purposes for their lives. In my silence I began to journal my more inner thoughts. As I was writing I found God saying to me "Surrender." Before I let him finish His thought I got quite upset, thinking *What else do You want from me?* Then when I gave Him the time He finished his thought "Surrender to My goodness."

Surrender and goodness had never gone together for me. They were like two kids from different sides of the track. Surrender had the connotation of giving up something I liked or wanted for something that was right but maybe not my first choice, at least initially.

Goodness on the other hand spoke to me of pleasure and childhood words and images like wonder, fantasy, and dreams. So when I heard "surrender to my goodness" I could not make sense of God's invitation to me. What is there to surrender to then? Especially because I had the inner sense that the word had to do with letting go of my role and walking away. I could tell by the agitation, waves of anger and sadness that I was experiencing during this time that something deeper was happening than I had yet grasped. This seemed to be the first piece of the puzzle revealing itself.

I arrived home later that day unusually sensitive to what was going on around me. It was as though the world moved into slow motion, giving me clearer insight into emotions, feelings and the impact of interactions going on between people.

After I tucked my children in bed and sent Maryanne off so she could have some time alone, I picked up a book I had wanted to read for sometime. It was a book given to me by a counselor I had visited at one point, trying to get an objective perspective on our journey. As I picked up this unassuming book and began reading it, in my acutely aware state of being, I felt like a child taking in all I was reading without adult filters of distrust and detachment. I was no further than twenty five pages into the book when a few sentences I had read were like the flip switch on a lever pulling out the support system holding up the shelf of my inner being. I buckled to my knees, groaning in pain. All of the thoughts I was reading were focused on one issue, one significant issue—my worth. They seemed focused around my need to be perfect, to have it all together, to present to God my own righteousness - earning His acceptance. I had been caught in the role of being the hero—the "messiah complex" and did not know how to be free.

I have no idea how my kids slept through my ordeal. For

some time I lay there groaning from the depths of my being. With my head now stuffed from intense weeping, I crawled into bed for relief. As I lay in my bed alone I felt a most unfamiliar sensation come over me or out of me, I could not tell. I could not identify the feeling. It was not sadness, anger or fear; it was unfamiliar. As the sensation began to overwhelm me, as though it had a "feel" and a "smell" to it, I felt alarmed. At thirty-two years of age, I was beginning to wonder if this was the feeling that took my father's life. I had not had suicidal thoughts before but would this experience lead to them if I let go into it?

The unfamiliar and uncomfortable feelings attached to this all-encompassing experience overwhelmed me. Maybe I could outrun it, I thought to myself, as though it might overtake me if I stayed still. I then realized I needed to cry out to Jesus for help. I knew I had to stay with it but why and how could I?

As the dread increased within me, I knew I had to let go into the experience. Speaking figuratively, it felt as though I needed to close my eyes and fall backwards as though I were high above the ground, believing Jesus would catch me. I somehow knew it was necessary to let go into the experience and to trust that God would be there. I eventually did.

Whether it took one hour or four, no recollection remains but that most unusual sensation subsided eventually. As I awakened the next morning I remember stepping out of bed only to feel like I had just lost twenty pounds from the core of my being. It was as if I had stepped out of bed only to land on the moon, defying gravity. At the same time, my entire abdomen felt as if I had just had surgery. My lower abdomen was so tender when I moved; it felt as if it had been incised clear across. For the next couple days I would be led by tenderness, tearful at the smallest of injustices committed against people.

In talking to a counselor and a psychologist friend I had more clarity on the content and context of my journey. I had never fully grieved my father's death. In fact I had spent over fifteen years avenging his death. My grief along with my unprocessed childhood pain was balled up inside me often driving me and controlling me without giving me rest. Though my pursuits were valiant I was driven by unprocessed grief. In that moment, the "lever" was pulled and grief was released, escaping me as though I was carrying something dead around inside me. The call to walk away and "surrender to God's goodness" dislodged this ball of grief and unprocessed pain. My identity was being wrapped up in what I did, my ability to perform, and my grief was keeping me there. I was not free to follow God because I was letting my identity get wrapped up in what I did and in my unprocessed grief.

Once I was free to follow and had surrendered to His goodness, we took the step of walking away from all we had known to begin again. I also walked away from being driven, and my wife will attest to that. Identity is an illusive thing until life dislodges our level of security.

Often men find that what they do defines who they are. Yet Jesus, long before he did any miracles, any healings, and any ministry had His Father speak His affirmation and complete pleasure over His life as a man. Jesus was on His way to the Jordan River to be baptized by John when He experienced the affirmation of His Heavenly Father publicly. The scriptures say that as He came up out of the water and a voice from heaven said "This is my son, whom I love; with him I am well pleased."[25] His worth and identity was in his belonging. He knew He belonged and He knew who He was outside of what He did. He knew He was the one His Father loved. Knowing our identity means knowing the ultimate issue of acceptance and love outside our roles or achievements. We are not free to follow and to fully live otherwise.

STAYING CONNECTED

We come to this place of passing on our journey to others only to discover we are still in process ourselves. We never seem to fully arrive, so how do we know when we have something worth giving? Our process and our journey are worth their weight in gold to those coming behind us and to those along side us. Our failures, our awareness of our incomplete identity, and our stories are invaluable.

It is the courage to be transparent and vulnerable concerning our process that qualifies us to pass on identity to others. Staying connected from generation to generation involves transparency and requires the use of story. Bill Carmichael in his book *Seven Habits of a Healthy Home* says, "One of the ways we pass on our legacy [and our process] is by telling stories...Bible stories, personal stories of faith, redemption, healing, personal crisis or struggles, and stories of the family."[26]

In the telling of story we become vulnerable, transparent and are able to connect with others where otherwise we might not. Image and imagination are powerful forces in our lives from the time we can begin to think and communicate. When you tell your story, you are not only communicating your legacy and [passing on identity], you are also helping yourself and your family shape life's message. Writer Sue Monk Kidd says, "Without such stories we cannot be fully human, for without them we are unable to articulate or even understand our deepest experiences."[27] Bill Carmichael writes, "By telling our stories, we recount and relive and reflect. It is a necessary way to help us find ourselves. When we tell stories, we create images in the minds of our listeners and take them places they have never been before. We invite them to share in our visions and landscapes. By telling our stories, we tell our listeners that we trust them to belong to us. As they enter our worlds, they become like kinfolk. A small piece of us is deposited in their memory and imagination. By exchanging our stories, we carry parts of ourselves into the other's legacy."[28]

I invite you to have the courage to stay connected so you can pass on identity by naming your next generation, as we would believe God would for the ones He loves. We join with the Mary's and Martha's of the past to call out to Jesus to come and find them and to find us. It is our privilege as communities of faith to enter into telling our next generation who they are - speaking into their doubt and affirming their identity by naming them.

We enter into their struggle as it is ours as well, to journey with them to find home, to find contentment with the unchangeable design of our lives. We enter into their search for identity with humility, encouraging them to find their worth outside of what they do. By telling them who they are, the ones He loves, we, too, enter into their game of hide and seek, realizing they have been waiting, desperately waiting, to be found.

Chapter 2
Process Questions

1. If being secure in God's love was on a scale of 1-10 (1 being low and 10 being high) how secure would you say you are in the love of God? Why would you say that?

2. What are some of the names and ways God has used people to "name" you in your life?

3. Have you taken the time to gain God's heart for others and "named" them? If no, why not?

4a. If the following defined the "unchangables" of your life, which of them would you least be at peace with
   • When I was born in history
   • Where I was born (country and place)
   • My family (Parents and siblings I was given)
   • My birth order (first born, middle child, etc)
   • My race and skin color
   • My gender
   • My physical stature
   • My physical traits(features)
   • My Personality and temperament
   • My talents and gifts

4b. Have you taken the area(s) you are least at peace with to God to settle it with Him?

5. How much of your identity is wrapped up in what you do rather than who you really are in God's eyes?

CHAPTER 3
LIVING FROM THE HEART

PASSION COMES FROM WITHIN

A community that commits to securing the identity of their next generation has taken the first step in the process of fathering. Knowing our identity, being completely loved by God, is really only the beginning. When one's passion is discovered through the life of community, the quality and purity of that passion is raised. In 1994 the world's attention had been drawn to a small and rather unknown village - Lillehammer, Norway. The attraction was the Winter Olympics.

Leading up to the events of this Olympics the coverage in the West or at least in North America was overshadowed by the bizarre media frenzy swirling around the women's figure skating competition. America's Snow White, Nancy Kerrigan, had been the center of an unusual and movie-like plot to maim her during the U.S Nationals, the irony being her perpetrator was discovered to be a teammate, competing for the U.S National Championship. Tonya Harding had paid someone to strike Nancy Kerrigan's knee during the competition, attempting to render her incapable of skating her performance. Though the blow to her knee was substantial it did not keep her from the competition.

Tonya Harding surprisingly not disqualified, participated in the Lillehammer Olympics, making for quite the made-for-television movie, which unfortunately overshadowed the Winter Olympics and the women's figure skating events. With all the elements of a good drama in place, the fight was over before it barely started. Early on in the women's technical competition, Tonya Harding's skate problems combined with other technical errors allowed Nancy Kerrigan to soar past her, easily securing first place in the standings.

With Tonya Harding far in the background and the story seemingly dead and the drama lost, we were yet met with another surprise. As Nancy Kerrigan entered the final skate—the women's artistic skate, she was clearly the leader. All she had to do was to skate a solid performance and the gold medal would be hers. It truly was an epic story of fairy tale proportions. The beautiful young maiden is plotted against by the jealous and envious witch, only to escape her grasp and prove she alone is beautiful and she alone deserves the crown. One could not have written the script for this any better, but who could have anticipated the turn of events to come?

Stepping onto the world stage, Nancy Kerrigan's skate was the best performance of her life, technically flawless and perfectly implemented. Every choreographed move was met with precision; every practiced skating jump and step was landed with complete confidence. Assured of the gold, Nancy Kerrigan awaited her marks and awaited the final skaters.

With all the media attention on the Harding-Kerrigan story many of the other skaters had been forgotten or missed along the way. One such skater was Ukraine's sixteen year-old orphan, Oksana Baiul. With a slight but completely unlikely chance for an upset, Oksana stepped on the ice for her final skate. With Kerrigan waiting and the skating world merely completing a routine, Baiul decided she had nothing to lose. With gauzes and bandages around her leg, from the morning skate where she had cut herself, she stepped onto the ice with only a dream in her heart.

In the first few moments of her routine the audience realized she was going to risk it all and give it everything she had. With the poise, presence and power of someone well beyond her years she captivated the audience and the judges. While clocking two technical errors during her skate she unleashed a most engaging performance, leaving the spectators breathless and the judges reeling. For a slight moment Kerrigan looked hesitant, but it was fleeting, while the tension was sustained.

As the world waited, the marks were lit up one by one on the scoreboard by the nine international judges. Each judge is to first give a mark from one to ten and then give an ordinal, the ranking of each skater against the others. The first eight judges revealed their marks, four rating Kerrigan with a number one ordinal and four rating Baiul with a number one ordinal. One judge remained. After an extended silence, holding the world in anticipation, the final German judge revealed his marks and ordinal, a number one ordinal for Oksana Baiul.

Baiul had won the Olympic Gold medal by the slightest of margins, 1/10 of a point, the closest score in women's figuring skating history. The world gasped in shock; Nancy Kerrigan looked on in disbelief. Unprepared for such an outcome, the Olympic Committee took twenty-six minutes to find the Ukrainian national anthem. The fairy tale was ruined. Or was another fairy tale being written?

Several months later I heard an interview with the very judge who placed the deciding and final ordinal. I was intrigued to hear his thoughts, his process and the influences on his decision. The interviewer asked him, "How did you make your decision? Why did you choose Baiul?"

I pondered his profound revelation for months. He said, *"Kerrigan's skating looked programmed, but Baiul's seemed to come from within."* He gave the final and decisive vote on one issue and on one issue alone—heart and passion. We may have all the talent and gifting that one could possess, but there is nothing like having heart. Nancy

Kerrigan, though technically perfect in this judge's eyes, lacked one thing—the most important thing: heart and passion. She landed a flawless program, something many of us only dream of doing in our field of skill and training, yet she still fell short.

We see this same story mirrored in another man's life, a man the Scriptures called the rich young ruler. *"A certain ruler asked him, "Good teacher, what must I do to inherit eternal life?"*

"Why do you call me good?" Jesus answered. "No one is good except God alone. You know the commandments: Do not commit adultery, do not murder, do not steal, and do not give false testimony, honor your father and mother."

"All these I have kept since I was a boy," he said.

When Jesus heard this, he said to him, "You still lack one thing. Sell everything you have and give to the poor, and you will have treasure in heaven. Then come, follow me."

When the man heard this, he became very sad, because he was a man of great wealth."[29]

The context of this story is primarily dealing with wealth, but the events of this man's life also carry a potent issue nestled inside all of us. This rich young ruler presented to the judge of all the earth (not just an Olympic judge), a technically perfect program. He kept the commandments, all of them so he claimed; he was flawless by the outward standards of the law. He choreographed the perfect performance, something most of us only dream of reaching. He kept all the requirements but lacked one thing spiritually, one vital thing—his performance looked programmed. Jesus recognized this by putting his finger on what was really inside him—the condition of his heart.

Jesus offered himself as master to this rich young ruler, and it turned out that money is what his real master was and what owned his heart. So when the state of his heart was exposed he was very sad, the scriptures say. This young man was hoping to gain the acceptance of God through his performance while overlooking his heart condition.

Like these two, there are many who seem more consumed with doing things right rather than being known for who they are. Being authentic, being who you are is part of realizing passion. We may not realize how easy it is to forget who we are and revert back to living a programmed life. Choosing to live life from a place of reaching for technical perfection rather than from the heart subtly overtakes us when our true passions are lost or unknown. In our busy and full lives it is easy to fall into meeting the standard, into trying so hard to be technically perfect for God, for people, for ourselves. It is especially easy if our heart has been misunderstood, hurt and bruised, or fearful due to unresolved pain. It is even easier if we have never known what it means to live from the heart.

As we think of our next generation, we have to think of their heart and their passions. Are they learning to live life from the heart or from technical perfection? Do we teach them to just be "good" people or to be "passionate" people? How are we training them to do life and how are we doing life? Valerie Bell in her book *Getting out of your Kids Faces and into their Hearts* says "We can't afford to 'fake' the way we relate to our children, by merely saying relational words suggested by 'experts.' Adjusting the words without adjusting the heart is a tempting relational shortcut – but one that can really backfire. It's like reacting to a bleeding wound with aspirin."[30]

THE NATURE OF THE HEART

When we speak of the heart, what is it that we are meaning? If passion comes from within and God wants us to follow Him from the heart, then what is the nature of the heart? From scripture we see that the Proverbs speak of the heart as a fountain of life. "Above all else, guard your heart, for it is the wellspring of life."[31] The heart is the place where life comes from, where dreams emerge; it is the sanctuary of humans, to be protected and guarded.

Jesus often likened the heart to a garden or to soil that needed nurture and tending. He described it as a place from which both crops and weeds can emerge. It is a home for sorrow and joy, ambition and humility and judgment and mercy. It is a place of deep tenderness and a place of monstrous rage. The heart is a place of mixtures. It is this capacity that confounds the wisest of men - its propensity for containing these mixtures or seemingly incompatible substances. Barbara DeAngelis, in her book "Real Moments", says, "Children are powerful seeds that grow up into gardens. What we plant into the mind and heart of one child will one day affect thousands of people." [32]

Growing up on the Canadian prairies I learned a lot about mixtures. Often it was during the cold winters when we chose to cut up firewood because the sap had drained itself from the trees, making the firewood desirable. The chain saws of that era often took a mixture of oil and gas in the fuel tank. Here it is, 30 degrees below zero, and the oil has spilled out of its container running down the sides of the bottle, blurring the instructions for the ratio of oil to gas. What is a teenage boy to do in such severe circumstances? That is obvious; simply guess at the mixture for the fuel tank. I knew I did not have it right when I started up the chain saw and clouds of blue smoke burst out of the exhaust chamber for some time. There is this same kind of mixture in the heart—dreams and passions of God and dreams and passions of our own making or our own brokenness.

Often our brokenness blurs our passions, distorting them unknowingly to us. The challenge is getting the mixture to reflect more of God and less of us, and it will always remain a mixture this side of Heaven. This is where community serves as a great asset. We may not recognize our own brokenness but others will more readily see it and can serve us by gently coming alongside us.

The challenge for every person comes in learning the struggle of mixtures without closing off the heart to others in the community during this process. *"The heart is deceitful above all things and beyond cure. Who can understand it?"*[33] On one hand the Scriptures refer to the heart as the wellspring of life, while on the other it can't be trusted because it is deceitful. Yet Jesus said to love the Lord with all your heart, with the new heart He has given us. How do we identify our true, God-given passions, finding a ratio that reflects a mixture of more of God than us? How do we find more of the new heart given to us and less of our old, crusty heart? How do we call out the true God-given passions of our next generation with certainty? First, we will always live with the mixture, yet our discernment will grow as we stay the course, learning to recognize God's passions from passions formed out of our brokenness. Our preparation benefits us and those intended to journey beside us, as they, too, will best discover their God-given passions in the place of community.

FINDING OUR REFLECTION IN THE MIRROR OF THE LIFE OF JESUS

"For whoever wants to save his life will lose it but whoever loses his life will find it." [34] The word used here for "life" is the same Greek word used in the Book of Colossians for heart. *"Whatever you do, work at it with all your heart, as though working for the Lord."*[35] In other words, to find our heart we often first have to lose our heart. To find what God's passions for our lives are, we first have to let go of our assumptions about them. We need to be willing to let Him change our heart or let other passions

grow in us. You can give it up willingly or have life take it from you, often in the most dramatic of ways. Giving it willingly, though not any easier, is met with less unnecessary pain.

I reached over to sign the contract, wishing I had never agreed to do it, but there seemed no other way out in my sixteen-year-old mind. You see, I had spent my whole life dreaming of being a professional hockey player. I loved the game of hockey as most Canadian boys do. All those 5:30 a.m. practices, the special meals, the hours of driving and training were about to pay off. My parents' investment of time and money was overwhelming. Yet this day was supposed to be the beginning of the reward for the sacrifice. I had been invited to attend a "Junior A" tryout camp, along with hundreds of other sixteen and seventeen-year-old dreamers.

The camp went well, and I gave it my best for the entire week. Yet the whole week I was wondering to myself, *Is this what I am really born to do?* I was passionate about the game of hockey, but was this God's passion for my life? Here was the first step of the rest of my life. Was God asking me to give it up for something else? For what?

With mixed feelings, I entered the room alone to receive my final evaluation with eight adult men. A few of them spoke, some read off charts, others communicated with eye contact. "Son," they said, "we like your moves; we think you have finesse and soft hands that could be developed further, and we want you to play for us."

I sat there confused, unsure of how to respond. I had lived my whole life to hear these words: *'You made it.'* Now somehow I was not sure I wanted to hear them. I sat for a few moments in silence, beginning to feel like this was not right, this was not for me, but how do I say No? With all the courage a sixteen-year-old could muster in the presence of eight intimidating men who only saw me as dollar signs, I said, "I can't play; my mother won't let me."

I don't know how it worked but it did and they let me go, but not without a contract. "Son, if you choose not to play we want you to sign with us so if any other team picks you up they will have to trade for you." I thought I don't want to do this, but if it will get me out of here I will sign. On that note I signed the contract and left for home, relieved and hoping I had chosen well.

One year later, with my last weeks of high school in view, I received a phone call. The voice on the other end said, "Hello, is this Todd Rutkowski?"

"Yes, that is me," I replied.

"Todd this is so and so from the Drumheller Falcons that you signed with last year."

"Yeah, yeah, good" I stuttered.

"Todd, we just wanted you know we acquired Wayne Gretzky's junior coach in the off season and with our exciting new management and staff we want to invite you to play with us this year."

I could not believe what I was hearing: *Wayne Gretzky's coach! You have got to be joking,* I thought to myself. *My passions or your passions, God—what is going on here?* My dreams were being reawakened after I thought I put them to rest. I stopped and prayed for a moment, asking God to help me.

In the flicker of a moment I just knew. I cannot explain it, but I just knew I was to say No and so I did. I willingly gave my passions to God, recognizing that He had other passions growing in me that would best reflect how I could live out His purposes for my life. I missed my hockey; there was no doubt about that, and at times I speculated on whether I had done the right thing. Of course, I have no idea if I could have made a career of hockey but I didn't pursue it to find out.

A few years later, while in living in the United States in

an area that had no arenas, I longed to play the game to which I had once given so much of my heart. So much so that I would put on my skates and run up and down the carpeted hallways of my college dorm just to experience that feeling again. Twenty years later I look back on that time in my life and I cannot imagine not having taken the path I chose. My God-given passions would not have been realized in the same way. My passions were too sketchy at that stage of the journey for me to have realized them. I am glad I trusted God when it did not yet make sense.

When we do not give up our heart willingly, it can often be a painful process, especially watching life take it from us or watching our success ruin us. As people face shattered dreams, or struggle with unmet ambitions, they struggle with the purpose to dream again. It can be like watching the plays of the month on the local sports channel. When the highlight reel is processing snapshots, it looks like surreal events pressed together, coming across your screen one after the other, undaunted and persistent in their drama. It leaves one overwhelmed, feeling the pain of it all. Yet even those who find success can find it empty and futile because it may not have been their God-given passion which they pursued. C.S. Lewis once said, "All that is not eternal is out of date."

We can see why people retreat back into living life in a programmed way because they can disconnect their heart to some degree by living that way. Technical perfection or meeting the standard is safer and less personal. It requires less of us, costs less, and protects our heart more certainly. Yet it often results in misery when we fail or discontentment and a lack of fulfillment when we succeed.

Living life from the heart and finding our God-given passions does not guarantee painlessness, however. In fact, it can often be far from pain free. Living from the heart can only guarantee that we are living life God's intended way, by living life with our spiritual ears open to His passions, rather than getting side-tracked to the safer road of technical performance or the deceptive road of passions born in brokenness. Good suffering and pain is walking life as He intended it to be. Bad suffering is trying to earn our love by perfecting a standard or gaining approval. Discovering our heart and passions involves seeing our reflection in the mirror of the life of Jesus. By identifying what His passions are, we become that much closer to the source of life and the dreams that are eternal, whether they bring pain or reduce it. What is it about Jesus that we—or those that we are journeying beside—love?

In the fourth chapter of the Gospel of Luke, we see Jesus alone and under deep distress from fasting for forty days. He stood at the precipice of temptation in His weakened state. He stood alone with no one watching, facing the most tantalizing of offers that appeal to our brokenness as humans: power, fame and prestige. He reached for none of them though He could truly have had them all. He would be owned by no one but His Father. He would do nothing for personal gain, but only serve the One who loved Him most. I love that about Jesus! His heart and passion was for God to be at the center of His choices, not His human ambition for fame, power or prestige.

We see how Jesus handled His disciples, how He taught them so creatively. He cared for them, He shared his life with them, and He made them stronger. He was not intimidated by their spiritual growth, but instead intentionally cultivated it. Yes, He became frustrated at times with them, and rightly so. Yet overall, He knew how to develop people, how to expose them to new experiences and new information, training them to evaluate those experiences so they could learn and grow. I love that about Jesus too. He invites people to grow.

In the Gospel of John, chapter eight, we see another part of Jesus as He was faced with the religious people of His day. The Pharisees, who were sometimes considered elders of the people, had caught a woman in the very act of adultery. With malice in their hearts they used her as a pawn to try to catch Jesus in a trap. Like hound dogs on a hunt, they stood before Jesus. With what looked like pieces of her dignity hanging from their mouths, they threw her into a public place at the feet of Jesus, awaiting His response.

Not intimidated by their trap, Jesus quietly knelt and drew in the sand with His finger. In the silence one could hear their heavy breathing, as they stood over her with stones in hand, anticipating the signal to pounce on their prey. Jesus responded masterfully to them, *"All right, stone her. But let those who have never sinned throw the first stones."*[36] With those words, their hearts were put on public display contrasted with Jesus' heart of grace. Mercy triumphs over judgment. This also, I love about Jesus. Rather than a thirsting for the blood of others because of their wrongs, Jesus is passionate about extending grace to them and freeing them from their addictions and sin.

What is it about the life of Jesus that stirs our passions? Is it His compassion for people or His concern for their practical needs, shown by His desire to feed the masses? Is it His ability to teach, to lead people to truth, or His willingness to serve others and embrace people unfamiliar to Him? Is it how He loved the unlovely or the way He protected and spoke up for the oppressed and marginalized? Was it His love of social justice, His willingness to confront injustice? Was it His worship of His father or how He made room for the next generation in His life and in His prayers? This is where finding our heart and passions in God begin, in the reflection of the life of Jesus.

THE MONSTERS UNDER THE BED

Moving away from living life by technical performance and standards of perfection starts us on the journey to finding our passions within. Once we move away from perfection, the next part of the journey for living life from the heart involves learning to live life from our God-given passions, which makes us vulnerable. As we start on this part of the journey we are often met with experiencing what it means to lose our heart to find it. We recognize how the heart is given to mixtures, mixtures of God's dreams and our dreams, and in the process of letting go of our dreams we often find His dreams for us.

However, as we walk down the journey to living from the heart we will also face *monsters under our bed*. As a child we may remember the proverbial monster under the bed. It was a way our parents could capture and define for us our fears of the dark and our fears of being alone as we fall asleep; the most vulnerable part of a child's day. In this journey that requires vulnerability, we face at least three types of monsters that try to keep us, and those we are journeying alongside, from our God-given heart and passions.

The question of heart and passion can be often found in the issue of unlocking our heart, not just discovering it, which is the first monster we meet under the bed of our lives. Life can be crushing or suppressing, either of which locks up our heart in fear. Fear of what others will think of us, or fear of losing friends or careers. Fear of failure, fear of the unknown or of trying new things, or fear of fear itself. Fear can lock up the heart and its God-given passions. A sense of injustice may well up within us, but since our heart is locked up in fear, that passion subsides like waves on the seashore, never to be expressed.

From base camp I could hear them talking over their

hand-held radios to one another as they searched for our lost team members in the cold November rain. We had been hiking in teams of six or seven for twelve hours in the Cascade Mountains in Southwest British Columbia when one team did not return before dark. It had now been close to eight hours since we had lost them and the search and rescue team we had called in had been unable to locate them. Due to the cold rain, the time of year and the lack of proper equipment, hypothermia was now of concern. With the sense of responsibility beginning to weigh me down, I was relieved to finally hear the words over the radio "We found them and they are alive".

I had been given the responsibility for developing and multiplying a four-day leadership training program for young people later referred to as the *"Niko"*, which originated in Hawaii with Jim White. The *"Niko"* process had some great elements but was still in raw form. In my opinion as a developer, it lacked clarity of purpose, a cohesive process, and multipliable materials and, as we discovered the hard way, increased safety mechanisms.

The vision of the *"Niko"* is to create an experience for the next generation to further discover their identity and purpose by *"overcoming"* within the context of community and within the raw ingredients presented by the untamed wilderness. The teams would be given difficult tasks that required physical, emotional and spiritual stamina that could only be accomplished outside their individual capacity. Learning to lean into God and one another is critical to the experience. The themes of surrender, servanthood and team leadership are experiences woven throughout the *"Niko"*.

After that cold November night, when we had lost four young people and two adults I was ready to let go of the *"Niko"* for good. Search and Rescue had found this team at one o'clock a.m. soaked to the bone, close to hypothermia, hiding together in a bear cave and lying in a pile to keep warm. One of the young people had their head cut open by a falling rock as well.

That morning the young people had been given topographical maps of their destination. Without adult supervision they were required to consider what supplies would be needed (food, matches, flashlights, etc) and to forge their hike through unmarked territory through the wilderness to their destination. Experiencing the consequence of their actions was immediate: no lunch, and walking in circles. It was a brilliant process, but now seemed too dangerous.

It had seemed like all our good intentions, all our passions for this had failed. Fear was closing in on us. I was fearful to keep developing the program as the cost of following this passion seemed too high. Over time a great team of people including Barry Watts, Les Derksen and others came alongside, enabling me to face my fears. The *"Niko"* became effective, safe and multipliable.

Since that time over ten years ago, the *"Niko"* has been developed and multiplied clear across the globe. It is being used by YWAM and churches everywhere to train young people in identity and purpose. What if we had stayed in our fears?

The second proverbial monster under the bed is the monster of pain. We cannot open ourselves to experience passion without opening ourselves to experience pain. Every expression of creativity risks being rejected. Every extension of kindness only hopes to be received. Every invitation of hospitality stands to not be welcomed and every dream dreamed can be threatened by disappointment and loss. When dreams die or are lost within us, they must be purged so new dreams can be conceived.

The doctor[37] responded with disbelief as the young Angolan woman answered his question for the third time in her native Bantu language. He continued speaking to her in

Portuguese, which she barely understood, much less spoke. Her response, which was translated to the doctor, assured him that she had not understood his question.

This doctor from America often volunteered his services in this war-torn and politically tumultuous land called Angola. Each year he traveled for weeks to Angola's northern Huambo Province, which was east of the capital Luanda, caring for the many neglected and suffering Angolans. With famine rampant and AIDS an epidemic, there was never a lack for his services. Having Portuguese ancestry contributed to why his humanitarian efforts focused on Angola. Portugal had been undeveloped herself and lacked the economic and industrial stability to develop her African colonies, especially Angola. Until late into the 1900s Portugal used the area around Luanda as a "slave pool" for her more lucrative colonies in Brazil.

After internal uprisings Angola received independence in 1975. Under the weight of civil war ever since and its instability, this doctor wanted to return to Angola whenever he could, since so much injustice had been done. Having been to the Northern Province many times in the past, he was well informed of some of the unusual physical defects and diseases. Yet when this lady had continued to respond to his question with the answer, "Yes, I am pregnant, I conceived nine years ago," he finally investigated with his own physical examination. He had seen this same lady the year before, dismissing her response the year earlier.

The question was, "You don't look pregnant but if you are, when did you conceive?" "How could she have been pregnant for nine years?" he wondered. Full of disbelief, he started the examination, expecting to find a tumor or some other mysterious disease. He felt a mass and decided to operate.

As he reached into her uterus, he felt something the size of his fist. Removing the tumor, he was struck with horror.

As he stared into his hand he saw a fully formed baby, completely calcified. For nine years she had carried this dead baby around in her womb. It had died there and remained. With the body unable to purge it, it completely calcified the dead baby to rock-like form in order to keep it. She was kept from conceiving again, living in bareness for nine years.

Though rare and unusual, this story poignantly illustrates the process that must take place when dreams die in us. Dreams are living entities. If the pain of their loss is not grieved and they are not purged from our souls, they remain like dead babies, calcified within us, disabling us from conceiving dreams and passions again.

The final monster hiding under the bed is the monster of dullness and hardness of heart. Like garden soil, the heart carries the inclination to hardening. A heart not regularly tended can build a crust over its surface or harden, making it impenetrable in time. As the proverb says, paraphrased, "Garden your heart with all diligence because out of it comes the dreams of God's heart."[38] The condition of our heart's soil is our responsibility, as the tools to tend it are God's. Often in our western perfectionism and our need to be "good" we exchange life and wholeness for resentment and obligation, which produce a hardness of heart in us.

In his book, *Soul Survivor*, Philip Yancey says, "Henry Nouwen had an affinity for paintings by his compatriots, especially Rembrandt and Van Gogh. He was especially fascinated by Rembrandt's painting *Return of the Prodigal son*. As he reflected on the parable of the *prodigal son* during his life, Nouwen found himself identifying most naturally with the responsible and obedient elder brother. Henry Nouwen was a Priest, Psychologist and Theologian. After his training he filled many ambitions by teaching at elite universities such as Notre Dame and Yale. He traveled widely as a conference speaker and had written sixteen books."[39]

Yancey says, "Henry Nouwen had done it all and achieved much but that was his very problem. His pressing schedule and relentless competition were suffocating his own spiritual life." His heart was hardening and a crust was forming over it. "He retreated to upstate New York for several months at a time and then withdrew to South America, scouting a possible role for himself in the developing world. He lived in a slum north of Lima, Peru in a parish of one hundred thousand people"[40], says Yancey. The children literally hugged life back into him, he would later say. "How little do we know the power of physical touch," wrote Nouwen during his sojourn to Peru.

Yancey describes, "After his return from South America he accepted a new position at Harvard University. However the pressures of fame, his teaching schedule and personal issues pushed him to the point of a complete breakdown within three more years. Later he fell into the arms of the L'Arche community, who work with the seriously disabled. Nouwen [was so moved by his experience that he] later asked for permission from his Bishop to join the L'Arche community"[41] in France. Yancey goes on to say, "For the first time in his life, he sensed God calling him to do something. He wanted to learn 'what seminary and theology didn't teach me: how to love God and how to discover the presence of God in my own heart.' Cast always in the role of a responsible elder brother, he had fallen prey to the very temptations that afflicted his prototype in Jesus' parable. 'The lostness of the resentful 'saint' is so hard to reach precisely because it is so closely wedded to the desire to be good and virtuous,' he declared." [42]

Henry Nouwen had been cast in a role in life that hardened his heart to his true passions and his hope was that by joining L'Arche community, for the first time these virtues might be realized. Nouwen wrote in his book *The Return of the Prodigal Son,* "I know, from my own life, how diligently I have tried to be good, acceptable, likable, and a worthy example of others. There was always the conscious effort to avoid the pitfalls of sin and the constant fear of giving in to temptation. But with all of that there came seriousness, a moralistic intensity—and even a touch of fanaticism – that made it increasingly difficult to feel at home in my father's house. I became less free, less spontaneous, and less playful.... The more I reflect on the elder son in me, the more I realize how deeply rooted this form of lostness really is and how hard it is to return home from there. Returning home from a lustful escapade seems so much easier than returning home from a cold anger that has rooted itself in the deepest core of my being."[43]

Henry Nouwen experienced a life of fighting off hardness of heart in order to live from His God-given passions. He discovered that being cast in the role of elder brother, though responsible and valiant to others, sometimes keeps us dull and unable to live from our God-given passions.

The provision for facing these three monsters is found in the healing, freedom and restoration given to us by the ministry of the Holy Spirit. Accessing that provision means accessing the presence of God within us and within the community of faith. We cannot tend our hearts alone; we need community, we need each other. Each of these monsters must be faced again and again as we learn what it means to live life from the heart. Facing these monsters can mean facing the community itself. The life cycle of birth, death and rebirth is part of the tension of living from the heart on this side of eternity. It is something we must learn how to embrace if we are to live life from the heart.

PASSION AND THE SALMON RUN

Each year the salmon of the west coast of the United States and Canada spawn. The locals refer to this amazing experience as the Salmon Run. Each fall thousands of ocean salmon, male and female, find their way up fresh water rivers, streams, and channels to the place of their birth. These fish transform their appearance into a stunning shade of red, which is the distinctive characteristic of a spawning salmon. Salmon between the ages of two and five find their way together, as male and female, to lay their eggs and to fertilize them.

In the fall of 1999, we took our three children—Megan, Keelan and Jayden— to experience the salmon spawn north of Chehalis, on the south coast of British Columbia. It was something none of us had ever seen up close. We watched in awe as hundreds and hundreds of salmon, resolute with intrinsic passion, were giving away their lives. Instinctively they swam up the river's bottom tracing their steps to their birthplace, to their death.

The channels they followed periodically displayed cascading waterfalls that produced turbulent waters, forcing them to leap over the canopy of falling water to continue their journey upstream. The narrow water shoots were integral to their completion. The extra oxygen needed to sustain strength was produced from the cascading rock face, creating white water.

Along the way we noticed hundreds, if not thousands, of salmon along the river's edge, dead, having given their life in the deposit of their eggs at their place of birth. It was an experience that left us speechless as we walked among the channels of the dead and of the yet unborn. Birth, death and rebirth: I was overtaken with emotion at the sight, realizing in that moment that the gift of life is to give life.

There is something about the salmon run that gives an account of the nature of passion. It is instinctive, intrinsic and comes from within. However, it is also filled with struggle. It needs the struggle to stay strong, to stay alive, and to make it home. It needs rugged obstacles to create the environment for that struggle to be sustained. Yet it demands the support of the community, fighting side by side, anticipating the future together. It requires a channel carved out ahead, making the destination accessible and reachable.

Passion is ultimately realized when home is revisited. For the salmon, it then gives away life for life's willing return. Passion is best discovered when we, like the spawning salmon, find our home. However, our home is in God. Once home is found, His unborn passions are ready to be birthed through us.

Chapter 3
Process Questions

1. How much of your life is living for technical perfection? (to be good, to please others, to perform and be accepted).

1b. What would those closest to you say?

2. Using a scale of 1- 10, (1 being low and 10 being high) To what degree are you living life from the heart?

3. What dreams and passions do you have in your heart that you have not yet given to God?

4. What dreams and passions has he given to you?

5. What "monsters under the bed" have affected your pursuit of living life from the heart?

CHAPTER 4
THE CRADLE TO THE GRAVE -
PURPOSE FORMED WITHIN US

THE POTTER AND THE CLAY

Identity and passion, though best discovered within the context of community, require an additional catalyst to be fully released. It is in the finding of our God-given purpose, within community, that a catalyst is created giving focus to our identity and passion. *"Go down to the potter's house and there I will give you my message. So I went down to the potter's house, and I saw him working at the wheel. But the pot he was shaping from the clay was marred in his hands; so the potter formed it into another pot. Shaping it as seemed best to him. Then the word of the Lord came to me, "O house of Israel, can I not do with you as this potter does?" declares the Lord. "Like clay in the hand of the potter, so are you in my hand, oh house of Israel."*[44]
Though our journey from the cradle to the grave is something we all share in common, sharing in the recognition of God's hand as the potter and us as the clay is uncommon. In His dialogue, vividly illustrating a relationship He has with us His creation, God depicted people as that lump of clay. In this passage God was speaking collectively and our application is individual and maybe diverting from Jeremiah's main agenda. However, the relationship portrayed, God as potter and we as the clay, allows us to see the individual and community characteristic of the relationship depicted, which is timeless and eternal.
Born into the world, impressionable, soft and moldable, our very existence speaks of our need to be shaped by the

Potter. Life invites us on a journey as we are marked by its experiences along the way, giving us our shape. We enter life as a lump of clay, fresh and unmarked, and depart kilned and fully formed. The fire of life and the touch of the Potter's hand shape us into our ultimate form and purpose. Watching the potter toil with the lump of clay on the potter's wheel allows us to enter into the sacred process from the standpoint of potter, shaping and reshaping, touching and then withholding that touch.

The commitment to this often-intense process is a combination of the masterful eye and the skilled hand of the potter connecting with the clay at the precise moment, to the right depth, for the precise length of time, shaping its distinctiveness. Our lives reflect the forming of purpose at the hands of the Potter—who jealousy moulds our clay.

When we are marred by life we must look for the hand of the Potter, who is longing to reshape us. Not every touch of life pressing against our clay can be attributed to God's direct connection, as evil also touches our clay. Yet every lump of clay created can respond to His shaping and reshaping, redeeming evil's touch.

Recognizing the hand of the Potter touching the clay is the first step to connecting with our purpose. Recognizing the hand of the Potter prepares us to come along side others who are in the journey with us. Often we can recognize God's hand on another's life more readily, allowing community to be unsurpassed as a place where purpose is most witnessed. To see oneself from another's perspective always reveals aspects of our "clay" that we do not see and maybe cannot see, from our perspective. When this reflection is conveyed in love, it can be very insightful and helpful. Often those coming behind us do not as readily recognize the hand of the Potter and need the perspective of those who have experienced more shaping to identify God at work.

IDENTIFYING SPIRITUAL EXPERIENCES

What is common to us all is not recognized by all. Jesus highlighted an uncommon reality of our world for us that revealed that heaven and earth are separated only by our blindness. *"The kingdom of God is near [you],"*[44] he said. The veil between this world and next, though very thin, often appears thick and unrecognizable to those who have not been trained to see it. The spiritual world all around us is teeming with God's life, waiting to touch us, to form us, wanting to break through the barrier between our spirit and the spirit of God. Though invisible, the unseen hand of the Potter reaches through the veil of eternity forming in us purpose, leaving marked trails of vision to those who perceive them.

Understanding how the invisible hand of God touches our lives involves training the eye to identify the Potter's work. Biblical spiritual experiences provide us with snapshots of the work in process. By placing the film from biblical spiritual experiences into storyboard form, we freeze the process, giving time for the eye to be trained to see the Potter's work in our lives. Through examining actual lives and experiences, we gain mental images of fully formed vessels, equipping us to recognize the work of the Potter.

In Genesis chapter thirty-two, we read the story of Jacob, who through the thin layer of eternity found God's hand reaching in and forming him, the clay. Jacob was on his way to meet his estranged brother when fear immobilized him. Hoping for the coming together of their hearts, yet preparing for the opposite, Jacob sent out a decoy. Anticipating retaliation, he sent livestock ahead as gifts in the hands of his servants, promising his brother he would soon follow, only to stay back another night.

During that night, anxious about the potential malice he

justifiably could encounter in his brother's heart, Jacob sent his wives and children across the river, remaining alone. The line separating heaven and earth dissipated, leaving Jacob in a surreal moment. In that instant, a Man whose existence seemed to straddle both worlds stepped fully into this world to wrestle with Jacob until daybreak. Though the lines between the two worlds seemed blurry, Jacob somehow knew he was wrestling not with himself or with another man, but with God. When it became obvious that the Man was not going to prevail against Jacob, he struck Jacob's hip, knocking it out of joint.

Covered in sweat from the night's struggle Jacob was losing his grasp on the Man's hand. In desperation he asked for a blessing as the man departed. The Man's response proved his identity. *"What is your name?"* he asked him. Jacob told him his name. The Man said, *"You will no longer be called Jacob. Your name from this day forward will be Israel."*

Jacob in turn asked the Man his own name. He responded without an answer and then departed, remaining nameless. Jacob later named the place Peniel, which means *"the face of God," for he said, "I have seen God face to face, yet my life has been spared."* [46] From that day forward Jacob, having been marked by the Potter, walked with a limp.

As we take the snapshots of this film that is frozen in time and separate them by placing them on a storyboard, we see the hand of the Potter at work in Jacob's life. Jacob was feeling vulnerable and unprotected. The props that previously gave him security, though false, were being removed as he faced the uncontrollable circumstances in his life. Jacob was in a season of desperation in his life. Anxious and afraid, he chose to be alone with God rather than meet his struggle alone. Putting himself in a place to meet with God, he invited the touch of the Potter, only to discover a struggle was necessary. He wrestled with his questions and his God, never receiving answers to his questions. Yet it was a memorable day, as he knew the hand of God had marked him. His clay had been partially formed by the struggle with his Maker. Our honest wrestling with God, like Jacob's, marks us forever. It shapes us and forms us.

When we allow our questions and our struggle to be placed in the arena of vulnerability and we allow our desperation to surface, we invite God into the ring to wrestle with us, forever changing us by the struggle. To stay out of the ring is to stay unmarked, unformed, and purposeless, yet to enter the ring is to risk the humbling experience of sporting a lifelong limp. We see many striking illustrations of people wrestling with God: Moses, David, Hannah, and Samson to name a few. Having all entered the ring of vulnerability, they wrestled with God, only to be marked by purpose in the process.

Not only are there times of wrestling that we willingly enter into but there are also spiritual experiences involving God's initiations towards us—not to wrestle with us but simply to touch us.

Moses was on the backside of the desert going about his own business when purpose found him in the most dramatic biblical illustration of God's initiation. Moses, while standing alone notices a bush bursting into flame, yet not being consumed. Intrigued by this phenomenon, he approached the bush naively. God, knowing He had gained Moses' attention, began to speak from the inner part of the flame. God's flame caught his attention but His words and presence pierced Moses' heart, forming his shape and purpose. It was in this moment, the moment of God's initiation, that destiny was revealed. Moses was being shaped to rescue a people from slavery. He was being shaped to free the very people he once enslaved. Uninvited and unexpected, Moses was being interrupted by the

Potter's shaping. God's purpose found him when he was not even looking.

I lay on my bed one night, wide awake and unable to sleep due to the events of that day. I had prepared myself through prayer and fasting for some planning meetings our leadership team was having about the future direction of our church. As the first day of meetings unfolded, we had considered multiple options for our growing community's future. Leading up to this time I had heard God whisper to me, "Be courageous."

As we began to clearly forge our direction, I could not settle with it, I could not embrace it fully. I knew that I needed to be courageous and speak out, but for a reason different from the one I had anticipated. Our team was an open and a safe place, and provided the climate to share honestly with one another, so I spoke my thoughts, which left me with more confusion than clarity as we ended our first day of planning.

The following morning we began to talk about what was in our hearts. When it came to my turn I could not speak. I was not ready, so I passed at that moment. However, my wife, Maryanne, did speak. One of the questions we as a couple had been wrestling with had to do with the idea of us planting another church. When asked where we were in that process, Maryanne blurted out, "It is not a matter of *if,* but of *when.*" Everything crystallized in her response for me. Church planting, that was it. My responses to the directions we were pursuing as a church were galvanized in that moment as I could now see how they were right for the church, but not for us in the long term.

Moments later we were affirmed in our response by the rest of the team. We were released now to think about church planting again. Yet that affirmation and permission to dream did not gain the response internally I had predicted. I was met with unanticipated emotion but that emotion was not excitement. I know the experience of faith being present and it was not there.

Having just pushed off from shore emotionally in speaking out courageously the day prior and now realizing the gift of faith was not at hand, I was set up for God's pottery work. I immediately plunged into a black hole of hopelessness, all within seconds. Though my outward appearance reflected differently from what I felt within, a member of our community discerned God's desire to touch my clay. They asked if they could pray for me. Before people had barely begun praying, I broke down. For about twenty minutes I wept in the presence of my friends. I had no idea why at the time. I was simply responding.

One of the other leaders present began to read to me the prayer of Isaac over Jacob in the book of Genesis. That prayer crystallized the nature of the void into which I had descended. I was receiving the blessing of my father— something I had never tangibly received. In my previous dramatic encounter with God around this issue five years earlier, it seemed He was cleansing me, yet this time it seemed He was filling me up with blessing. He was filling a void. This time I was getting the blessing of my heavenly Father, the one I needed most. Every word from Genesis twenty-seven was like a word directly from God's heart to my heart. In that instant I received a spiritual transfusion. It was as though abandonment was being displaced by blessing in my spiritual veins. I went home that night acutely aware of the spiritual world.

The curtain between God's spirit and my spirit was very thin that night. I could feel His presence like a gentle blanket surrounding me. My spirit and God's spirit were communicating intensely and freely. In the flash of a moment revelation struck me. My life was like Jacob's. My mother's faithfulness was comparable to Rebecca's, Jacob's mother. The blessing I was receiving that day was because of the faithfulness she displayed in crying out to God for her fatherless children.

I began to weep, impacted by the gratefulness I felt towards her. Then God took me further into the story of Jacob, only to leave me with these words. "Today I have given you Leah but it is Rachael that is in your heart; if you will wait for her, I will give you Rachael."

I knew that in that moment I was to stay a while longer and I sincerely could serve from my heart now. Jacob had wanted to marry Laban's daughter Rachael. However, Leah was older and culturally must be married first. Jacob, though expecting Rachael, received Leah as his wife first and was required to wait longer for Rachael, whom he truly wanted to marry.

I knew we would be planting a church again, but not yet. The next day I remained tender and close to the presence of God, Who was profoundly touching my clay and forming His purpose within me. Each time, over the next several days that I reread Genesis twenty-seven, I wept again, as though blessing was being poured into my soul. I realized in those times I had been touched by the Potter's hand.

Joshua, Moses' disciple, was on his way to the city of Jericho when he saw a man standing in front of him with a drawn sword. As a man of war in a time of war, Joshua hesitated, uncertain of the identity of this unfamiliar person. In determining the status of this stranger Joshua asked if the man was for him or for his enemies. Joshua was met with the most interesting of responses, especially in a time of war, where people are either with you or against you. "*Neither,*" the man said, "*but as the commander of the Lord's army I come.*"[47] Joshua, quick to recognize Whom he had just met, fell down on his face in worship. The man said to him, "*Take off your sandals for the place where you are standing is holy.*"

God did not come to first give Joshua direction or to tell him to do something. He came to mark his clay, to touch him and remind him to Whom he belonged and to Whom he served before He gave him direction. He initially left no visible instructions until Joshua's worship was expressed. When God did give direction to Joshua, it was bathed by the mark of their closeness making way for its reception.

There are times in our lives when God draws close to us, when He seems nearer than at other times. For no apparent reason initially, the veil that separates this world from the next grows extra thin. In those moments, the gentle hand of the Potter is coming to form the clay. He is coming to touch us and to change us by first of all simply being close to us.

On other occasions, we are harshly struck by the intensity of the hand of the Potter in His discipline of us, shaping us by His demonstrative grasp. The writer of Hebrews captures the essence of discipline that shapes us. *"My son, do not make light of the Lord's discipline, and do not lose heart when he rebukes you, because the Lord disciplines those he loves and he punishes everyone he accepts as a son."*[48] Though male in orientation, the principle is genderless. Those he loves, he forms through discipline, male or female.

While discipline is different than punishment, they don't always feel different in the moment. Punishment is the response for wrong doing, while discipline is a response for life and growth. Whether we are working out in a gym or following through on our previous commitments, discipline is often required to sustain the outcome. Often it is the deception of life that our pride chooses to disguise. Loving discipline must first confront the deception within us. Discipline comes to us through people, through life's circumstances and through our self-induced blindness, often leaving us shocked and numb initially. Punishment is often the result of us not responding to discipline.

In II Samuel 12 in the Scriptures, we read about the story of King David who was disciplined by his own sin in a shocking discovery, which was only realized through the telling of another's injustice. Nathan, a friend of God and a friend of David, served to restore their broken relationship through the process of discipline. Having the trust of both God and David, Nathan was allowed to gain access to David's heart. Nathan told David a story of injustice, capturing David's response and using it to catch him. David's response to the injustice enacted in Nathan's tale revealed the severity of David's own injustice. As Nathan continued to solicit David's reaction, he informed him that the main character in his story was actually David, the one who performed the injustice. David in this moment was deeply pressed by the hand of the Potter and the hand of his own sin, making a memorable indent in his clay. It was not his sin but his response to his revealed sin that allowed the Potter's hand to mark the clay.

King David had stayed home from war only to become distracted by a beautiful woman. He invited her to his home and slept with her while her husband was at war on his behalf. Discovering she was pregnant, David sent for her husband immediately. David anticipated that Uriah would sleep with his wife if adjourned from the battlefield, a perfect disguise for David's sin.

Yet Uriah would not go home to his wife while his fighting men stayed in the battle on his behalf. Uriah's honor thwarted David's schemes, sending David's heart further into the abyss of injustice. Her husband's death was all that was left to ensure that David's sin remained hidden. David took advantage of the kingdom entrusted to him, having Uriah sent to where the battle was fiercest. Placing him against the city wall where the enemies' strongest fighting men were stationed secured David's wicked plot of having an honorable man die an honorable death.

David culminated his scheme by taking Bathsheba as his wife, giving credence to her pregnancy. With his scheme solidified and David exhausted from hiding his sin, he could now shut the door to his sin and throw away the key forever. However, Nathan pulled the mask off David's disguise. God worked through Nathan to discipline him by opening David's calloused heart to his sin. In that moment David's clay was shaped and formed by God's discipline because David chose to receive it.

Spiritual experiences found in the scriptures seem at times to be a respecter of race, age or class. The scriptures portray that the poor, the marginalized and the youngest, see the *Kingdom of God* often before the rest. The scriptures indicate that God favors the young and the lowly, indicating that in their presence we will see His hand more obviously. Yet God invites us all to walk towards the thin veil between heaven and earth, inviting him to form and shape his purposes within us.

RECOGNIZING GOD'S PREPARATION IN OUR LIVES

Our lives reflect the deposits made by God, which display His purpose through our lives. We all have been given a tailored training program, which includes the formal and informal aspects of preparation. Many of us have not seen how God places our future in our past. Often our lives are uncut, not capable of reflecting His purpose and beauty. The informal part of the process involves recognizing facets of the character of God entrusted to our lives. Our lives become like facets of a diamond, displaying His character. Taking an uncut diamond and faceting it, at the right angle, will make light refract through the stone in such a way as to show the most brilliance, making it beautiful. While refraction, which is the bending of light through the diamond, is part of faceting, dispersion is another factor that affects faceting.

Dispersion is the splitting of white light into spectral properties. Diamonds have a very high dispersion, so we see colorful flashes in a colorless stone when it is cut at the correct angles. The hardness of the stone plays a role in the cutting of diamonds as well. A softer stone will cut quickly, requiring gentleness in the cutting process. Refraction, dispersion and hardness are all properties that affect the faceting of diamonds, ultimately affecting the display of their beauty.

We are uncut diamonds, mined from the earth of our sinful natures. We, like the diamond, reflect light, God's light. The properties of refraction, dispersion and hardness have similar bearings in our ability to display God's intended beauty through our lives. The facets of our lives when cut at the right angles refract through us, displaying His character. When the dispersion is accurate we see colorful flashes of God's character in our colorless stone. God's faceting involves an assessment of our hardness, being gentler with those who are of a softer property. What are the uncut aspects of the character of God entrusted to our lives?

He was not a big man, nor a handsome man for that matter, but his impact on the world has historically left him standing tall and displaying attractiveness greater than his own. Paul, one of the legendary influences on the early Church and one of the most prolific writers of the New Testament, was not known for his Hollywood appearance or his athletic build. Rather he was a colorless stone reflecting colorful flashes of the character of God. Once considered a murderer and a persecutor of Jesus, he later became the apostle of mercy. Paul refracted the mercy of God through the faceting of his stone. He was cut in such a way that the light of God's presence displayed the beauty of mercy through his life. God cut Paul aggressively because his properties were hard. God struck him blind on the road to Damascus drastically faceting Paul's uncut stone. Paul often referred to himself as the chief of sinners, which indicated the level of mercy he had received. Because great mercy had come to Paul, mercy could be refracted through him.

John, spoken of in the gospel of John and the epistles of John, displayed the beauty of God's love once it refracted through him. One of John's encounters with Jesus was through his mother. His mother requested for Jesus to make room for her two sons at His side when He reigned as King to avoid any shame coming upon John if her request was denied.[49] In a society of honor and shame one must avoid shame, and her indirect request on his behalf would ensure shamelessness as John was already being apprenticed to Jesus. Yet her request on his behalf reflected his ambition. John, in his uncut form, proved to be filled with ambition that had the appearance of godliness at times. Presumptuously he protected justice, by wanting to call fire down from heaven on people who were not responding to Jesus. [50]

Yet John later became known as the apostle of love. When faceted by God, John refracted the light of God to display the essence of His love. The properties of refraction, dispersion and hardness all play roles in the various aspects of the character of God reflected through our lives. Though there are many aspects displayed through us we seem to be predisposed to having dominating aspects or what could be viewed as major and minor reflections of His character through us.

Little did I know that as I stood to speak at my father's funeral that I would be speaking something that would later reflect the character of God that would ultimately be displayed through my life. Being only fifteen years of age contributed to the innocence and courage I had in that moment. For my father's funeral that day, I found myself unusually resolute. Days earlier I had lain on my bed thinking about what had just happened to my life, my father and to my world. I lay there, thinking there was only one possible response to this tragic event.

It was actually quite simple to my teenage mind when I look back on it now. If the torment of my father's guilt and sin allowed the enemy free access to further torment him, driving him to the depth of despair, required for one to take his own life, then surely I must give my life completely to God. Who else but God could deliver justice for his death? The enemy of his soul and mine tormented him and took him prematurely. I could not give my life to him or his ways—bitterness, hate and rebellion.

I had one option. Giving my life to God and asking him to utilize it to advance His purposes on earth was the only thing that made sense. Having settled my response to my father's death, I had one last wrong to right. I needed to speak for him since he could no longer speak for himself. I wanted the people at his funeral to know that he was a seeking man who, though deeply tormented, had finally found peace with God. And though he found peace, he was unable to escape the grasp of shame and find an end to his addictions.

Though I spoke at his funeral that day I am left with no recollection of my words, only my intent. The hope refracted through my life that day spilled over to those around me, framing God's reflection through my life. As God was radically faceting my life, He dispersed His light through me allowing my colorless stone to display His colorful flashes. My life's purpose was to become clearer at a later date, though it was first refracted in my life at fifteen. My life would become a reflection of hopes and dreams.

So what has He entrusted to each of us of His character?

As we look around the community and to those coming behind us, what aspects of His character do we see in raw and uncut form in the lives of others that we can encourage?

Istanbul, built across two continents, was at one time the eastern center for the Roman Empire and was formerly known as the legendary Constantinople. Stationed on the shores of the Bosphorus, Istanbul boasted the largest enclosed space on the face of the planet for over millennia, Hagia Sophia. The longest surviving work of the Byzantine architecture was first built in the fourth century as a church. After a fire in 404 A.D and again in 532 A.D, it was replaced by a second church. The existing structure was primarily erected between 532 A.D and 537 A.D during the reign of Emperor Justinian. It was the church of both the Emperor and the Patriarch, making it the place where most of the religious and state ceremonies were held.

After nine hundred and sixteen years Hagia Sophia in all her grandeur was converted to a mosque in 1453, shortly after the conquest. Apart from whitewashing many of the paintings and mosaics and the removing of religious symbols, the Turks left Sophia relatively untouched. In 1935 Sophia became a museum.

Turkey was a Muslim country in 1992 when Maryanne and I and our sixteen-month-old baby Megan, arrived in Istanbul. Allured by the city's mystique, we searched the 7500 square meters of Sophia's grandeur, intrigued by the wealth of history she contained within her walls. In the upper gallery I was drawn to a faded mural that had remained etched into the walls for over fourteen hundred years. From a distance the outline and silhouette was distinct and recognizable. Each step I took towards the image enhanced its imperfections and highlighted its fading; the impact of aging over centuries. The closer I got to the image the more I lost its form and shape. Standing directly in front of the mosaic I was awed by the thousands of tiny cubes that made up this larger image of Christ. Some of the cubes appeared insignificant up close; others were obviously faded, yet all were defined by their distinctiveness. All of the cubes were necessary, offering perspective only from a distance.

We are all cubes providing a small perspective of Christ, a more complete picture when we are viewed together. Though we will each display and reflect part of His character to the world around us we must recognize that it is only in community, which crosses generations, that we can fully display the multifaceted character of Jesus. This mosaic of Christ has been observed in succession for over fourteen hundred years, allowing it to be seen by each generation. So too, every living generation has the opportunity to connect together to display Christ.

We are born into this world with a color and texture that defines our influence as human beings. We enter the world covered in a transferable influence that can be passed on to others like wet paint. Some of the colors we touch dry and remain a part of us throughout our lives. We are all born bearing different colors, different textures and different volumes of paint, yet we are all changed by the wet paint of others encountered along the way.

Some of us are born with bright neon colors, others earthier tones and yet still others in pastels. Some of our textures are gritty, some satin and some in full gloss. Yet we all have a color and texture, defining our influence.

Learning to discern the influences upon our lives more readily helps us determine God's preparation for purpose. Who has He brought into our lives along the way to form us? Who has contributed their color to ours?

For most of us, it starts with our mothers. We for the most part carry the color of our mother in our lives, but what other colors have been added? Even people who may have been ungodly or possibly evil can leave a redemptive capacity in our lives through their influence. Assessing the deposits of those whose colors we bear begins to give us a greater understanding of God's informal preparation in our lives.

In my life there have been threads of influence that have touched my life forming purpose within me. Several significant women have poured into my life, enhancing the feminine aspect of my leadership style. Primarily people who are pioneers and developers have either touched me with their color or I have been attracted to theirs. I have been influenced by the paint of diverse cultures, affecting my color significantly. The paint of global thinkers and innovators has touched me and remained. The paint of deeply spiritual people who have encountered Jesus has found its way to mine. Through recognizing the thread of influence poured into my life, purpose has become more crystallized.

Ask yourself, Who has poured into my life, and to whom am I pouring into? Recognizing the informal training in our lives brings us closer to discovering the purpose intended for our lives. Finding out what aspects of God's character have been entrusted to us, while identifying themes of influence painted upon us, forges a path through the raw elements of purpose, making God's purposes in our lives clearer.

HAVE YOU BEEN TO THE DESERT LATELY?

Jesus witnessed God's strength in the desert; Paul found revelation in the desert, and John the Baptist was prepared in the desert. Moses fled to the desert and Abraham freely walked towards it. Desert time is a common experience in the forming of purpose. The desert is a paradox of sorts. Desert time is a time in our lives where God seems far away and distant, cold and unreachable yet at the same time he becomes nearer, more distinct and more accessible in the end. It is a time when we are tested and confronted in the core of our beings.

In the desert people's efforts to comfort us seem futile, often complicating our already perplexing reality. Yet the most compelling feature of the desert is that though we are around people, we are painfully and awkwardly alone. We find no explanation for how we arrived in the desert, yet we are acutely aware we have arrived. We feel incredibly alone, alone with our thoughts; as though a glass wall were placed around us, keeping us from touching others and being more ready for God. Initially in the desert God is silent, though His former words stir inside, testing us to our core.

The dry and sweltering heat of the desert contributes to the pressure building within us from the silence, eventually surfacing every fracture and crack in our trust of Him. The desert can come to us in the form of physical pain, emotional pain or spiritual pain, and when it comes there is no mistaking of unjust pain.

Given the choice, we would avoid the desert. But why would we, really? Subtly underneath our avoidance of unjust pain is the fear that pain marks us in a negative way. This fear grips us, trying to give weight to the belief that we are flawed by pain and therefore we are best off avoiding the desert. Often we see unjust pain as though it is the enemy of God or at least more powerful than God. We react to it as though painful experiences thwart God's purposes for our lives. In her book, *Praying for Rain—Surrender and Triumph in Life's Desert Places,* Nancie Carmichael writes, "The deserts of our lives are creative places. I've learned that the desert is not a tragedy. What is a tragedy is not to hear what God was saying to me there."[51]

It is in the desert where we are tested and solidified. It is in the desert that purpose is tried and conviction is formed. It is in the desert that we meet God in ways we could have otherwise never experienced. Though difficult at the time, desert experiences often prove to mine the depth of God's love, making a deeper deposit within us. The Swiss psychiatrist Paul Tournier wrote, "If anything is certain, it is that every one of life's trials, if only because it breaks the hard crust of our physical and mental habits, creates, like the ploughing of a field, an empty space where seed can be sown. In the sudden void caused by bereavement...an illness...failure...loneliness...your mind is assailed by fundamental questions to which you hardly ever gave a thought in the coercive whirl of life."[52]

Intertwined into the issue of unjust pain is the question of God's favor. We know at least in part, that we are loved by God. In many ways that is the problem we have in our attempts to relate to God on this matter. He loves everyone indiscriminately, even those who will spend eternity apart from Him. The real question that comes out of unjust pain is the question, not of love but of favor. Does God approve of me? Am I still pleasing to him?

At Jesus' baptism the words of His Father spoken from the cloud straight to Him address these two issues separately yet simultaneously. *"This is my son, whom I love; with him I am well pleased."*[53] Jesus needed to hear He was loved and that He was pleasing also. You can love someone with whom you are displeased. When we step in the desert, we are faced with this question, the question of favor. Unjust pain, it seems, draws out any unanswered questions relating to the favor of God in our lives.

In the life of Job, the issues of unjust pain and favor surface and play the role of a teacher if we choose to listen. The book of Job opens by introducing Job as a blameless man, full of integrity. Not a guiltless man, but a blameless one. A blameless man is not merely someone who has not done wrong but one, who no matter how horrible the offences committed, has had the charges against them removed. No blame is attached to him because the One offended has exonerated him. To be blameless, as Job has been presented to us, meant he trusted in the Lord's faithfulness and covenant, not his outward conduct. This blameless man was about to experience some of the most horrific pain a human could face, the loss of a child.

In one day, one very evil day, thieves and bandits stole Job's livestock while slaying his servants. Simultaneously a tornado struck his children, who were gathered for a meal at the home of his eldest son, destroying all of them and the house. Job immediately was plunged into the desert, tempted to question God's favor in the coming days. He was tempted to let go of his belief that God approved of him. During that time Job groaned, he wailed, he doubted and fell into depression. At times he lashed out like a wounded animal. Yet he remained blameless. He did not allow his pain to undermine the sense of God's favor on his life. Job violently resisted the idea that there must be something else he must do to gain God's favor in the adverse circumstances pressing down on his life.

Every parent who has experienced the pain of a straying child knows of what I speak. Every child who has been haunted by the betrayal of a parent knows all too well of what I speak. Unjust pain unearths the question of favor within us. We fear pain because we fear it will take from us our blamelessness before God and stamp us as unapproved. Yet the Book of Romans provides us with God's perspective on the place of unjust pain in the lives of those who are blameless before him, *"For we know that all things work together for good to those who love God and are called according to his purpose."*[54]

Unjust pain, though it tries to undermine our grasp on God's favor is a reality we all, Christian or non-Christian, experience in our broken world. Unjust pain is not a respecter of persons; rather it often is an extension of an interconnected sinful world. Unjust pain is not able to stamp us unapproved or hinder God's purposes for our lives unless we let it.

As blameless people, exonerated by God, we must recognize that it is our response to unjust pain in the desert that we must guard against, not the pain itself. Job discovered that to be true. *"But he knows where I am going. And when he has tested me like gold in a fire, he will pronounce me innocent."*[55] Unjust pain cannot steal purpose; it can, however, form it.

PURPOSE FORMED WITHIN US

We end where we began, back on the Potter's wheel. From the cradle to the grave God is forming His purpose within us. As He places our lump of clay on His potter's wheel He does so with great delight. He knows the process will have moments of great joy and great sorrow. He is aware that at times we will lose sight of the journey and fight against His initiatives. At other times He will tightly grasp hold of us squeezing in purpose through discipline. He will offer his presence to us along the way anticipating our invitation to let Him come close and touch us. He will remind us, on occasion, that the veil is thin and that He is so very near us, wanting to whisper purpose to us. He will bring people into our lives along the way to be part of faceting us, permitting His character to refract through us.

Community, when welcomed into our lives, will take the role of partnering with God in faceting, depositing influence, and providing perspective in the shaping process. Some of our relationships will transfer their color and texture upon ours while others will simply model purpose to us.

Our purpose will only be realized in community; in that place that we find our cube, in that living mosaic of Christ.

Finally, He will form us in the heat of the desert where truth will be tested in the pain of injustice. It is the testing that propels truth's descent from the head to the heart, bringing into being conviction, which is the cornerstone of purpose. From the cradle to the grave, His purpose is being formed within us at the hands of the Potter. If only we were more aware, if only we were more visionary, what might it contribute to our lives and to the future generations? What could occur if a purposeless generation recognized that purpose was subtly being formed within them?

My story is that story, a tale of identity, passion and purpose being formed within me in at the hands of God through community. As an abandoned teenaged boy, prematurely cut off from being fathered, various men and women stepped into my life in different ways and at different times to name me, often speaking my identity to me unknowingly. Many from within the community made room for the fledgling expressions of passion stirring within my heart.

The community, though changing throughout the seasons of my life, unknowingly served together to prepare me to recognize the hand of the Potter forming His purpose within me. It was the many, not just the one, who contributed to passing on identity, passion and purpose, attesting to the power of community in fathering my life. *"He turns a wilderness into pools of water, and dry land into watersprings. There he makes the hungry dwell, that they may establish a city for a dwelling place. And sow fields and plant vineyards, that they may yield a fruitful harvest."*[56]

Chapter 4
Process Questions

1. Name the ten most influential people (good or bad people) in your life?

2. Can you identify any common themes or threads between those people? (musicians, gender, race, gifts, passions, etc)

3. What spiritual experiences have happened in your life? (Wrestling with God, God's initiation to come near you, direction, healings, deliverance, discipline from God) What has formed in you as a result?

4. Who are you becoming? What characteristics of the character of God do you see being refracted and dispersed through your life (whether in matured or raw form)? (Love, compassion, justice, power, faith, childlikeness, mercy, generosity, gentleness, strength, peace, etc.) Ask others what they think.

5. What desert experiences have you had in your life? How have they shaped you?

6. Name up to five "losses" in your life? Do you see how God has used those to touch or encourage others? If not why?

CHAPTER 5
WHEN OUR REACH
EXCEEDS OUR GRASP

WHAT SIGNIFICANCE IMPLIES

Martin Luther King Jr. once said, "One of the most agonizing problems within our human experience is that few, if any, of us live to see our fondest hopes fulfilled."[57]

If attaining our dreams and purpose defines our significance, most of us live out our lives in insignificance. If we do attain our dreams, it is often not without the constant reminders seen in the carnage of disappointment and failure strewn along the path of our lives. If we did not feel significance was about attainment, we would not be devastated by failure, which often leads to disappointment. To function in the reality of failure we need to understand how to interpret the relationship between failure and significance.

The message sent to us by the school system, the work force and society at large is that a person who fails is insignificant. If failure is defined as not achieving something, then most of us live within the reality of continual failure. Most of us never fully attain what we are looking for or what we are reaching for in life. Often we learn early on in life to stop looking so hard or reaching too far to avoid being disappointed. So how do we understand disappointment and failure?

We must first recognize that failure is not the person; it is an event that should not be connected to our significance. How many of us really believe that? Failure on this side of eternity is inevitable, so how do we live with it? How must we view failure if we are to search for identity, passion and purpose in our existence? How are we to struggle with it in community and in supporting those coming behind us as they take risks that land them in the center of failure?

Hebrews chapter eleven introduces us to what some call the "hall of faith." It is the chapter that names those whom the Scriptures have honored for their trust in God and their reward of attainment. The headliners in this chapter are Abel, Enoch, Noah, Abraham, Isaac, Joseph, Moses and Rahab. However, as we come to the close of the chapter, we read words that challenge our beliefs if we believe that we must attain something to find significance and meaning. *"And what more shall I say? I do not have time to tell about Gideon, Barak, Samson, Jephthah, David, Samuel, and the prophets, who through faith conquered kingdoms, administered justice, gained what was promised; who shut the mouths of lions, quenched the fury of the flames, and escaped the edge of the sword; whose weakness was turned to strength; and who became powerful in battle and routed foreign armies. Women received back their dead, raised to life again. Others were tortured and refused to be released, so that they might gain a better resurrection. Some faced jeers and flogging, while still others were chained and put in prison. They were stoned; they were sawed in two; they were put to death by the sword. They went about in sheepskins and goatskins; destitute, persecuted and mistreated. The world was not worthy of them. They wandered in deserts and mountains, and in caves and holes in the ground. These were commended for their faith, yet none of them received what had been promised."*[58]

There were those named in this "hall of faith" who knew nothing more than apparent failure on this side of eternity. Their lives were marked insignificant by the standard of attainment. None of those mentioned in the latter part received the promise. They lived always expecting and never experiencing the fulfillment of their fondest dreams. They never completely experienced their identity, passion and purpose in this life. Yet the writer calls them those *"whom the world was not worthy."*[59] They were graded by a different system. Their lives, while considered significant to God, were marked by disappointment, failure and insignificance by another grading system. This chapter in Hebrews poses a different criterion for our definition of significance.

Significance in God's heart is in no way connected to the attaining of something. We clearly see that significance is connected to 'being' and being is joined to our centeredness in God. Being centered gives us the capacity to hang onto a hope that may never be attained. While "our reach [often] exceeds our grasp", says Dr. King[60], God commends us for reaching. He himself is a God who reaches and yet sometimes does not attain, especially in the confines of relationship with us.

THE OBSTACLE OF DISAPPOINTMENT AND FAILURE

As we put the fragmented pieces of Paul's own struggle together (spoken of in his letter to the Romans in the New Testament), we gain a compelling illustration of the problem of disappointment and failure. We see depicted in Paul's own life what it means for someone, sold out to living out his identity, passion and purpose, to not receive the promise or at least parts of the promise—even the promises of God. We can quickly see in Paul's letter to the Romans his intent for going to Rome and then on into Spain. *"So from Jerusalem all the way around to Illyricum, I have fully proclaimed the gospel of Christ. It has always been my ambition to preach the gospel where Christ was not known, so that I would not be building on someone else's foundation. Rather, as it is written: 'Those who were not told about him will see, and those who have not heard will understand' this is why I have often been hindered from coming to you. But now that there is no more places for me to work in these regions, and since I have been longing for many years to see you, I plan to do so when I go to Spain."* [61]

Paul, knowing who he was and what his purpose was, had a passion to go to Rome and then on to Spain. His purpose for going was unmistakable in this passage. He wanted to bring the Romans a spiritual gift, and he wanted to extend the good news to the expanding edges of the advancing kingdom of Christ to Spain. With passion and purpose in his spirit Paul penned these words as though they were not only his dream but the will of God, *"You are in my prayers at all times; and I pray that now at last by God's will the way may be opened for me to come to you. I long to see you, so that I may impart to you some spiritual gift to make you strong."* [62]

Yet Paul never saw Rome in the way he had anticipated. What he saw of Rome he saw through the eyes of a prisoner, not of a free man. The people of Spain likely never boasted of Paul's presence in their city as his passion and sense of purpose indicated. Even his journey to Rome had detours along the way, a two-year stop in a Caesarean jail and a shipwreck on the Island of Malta in the Mediterranean Sea. Paul was faced with the agonizing mark of disappointment and failure on his life. Would this apparent failure mark him as insignificant along with his previous marks of apparent failure?

Before Paul met Christ personally on his Damascus road experience, he thought he was serving God by persecuting the first Christians. He was convinced that he was carrying out a successful crusade by wiping out Jesus' followers, only to discover that what he defined as *success* was actually a tragic failure. He learned that things are often not as they appear. We, like Paul often attach the tag of *success* to things God would call failure and the tag of failure to what God would call *success*. Our incessant pursuit of materialism, power and pleasure, symbols of success in our society, are not as they appear. When you read the history books and search the lives of people who lived with passion and purpose, very seldom was their significance defined by material possessions, pleasure seeking or power. Often you have no idea of these elements, as it is not how success over time and in eternity is measured. Paul's life—as does ours—had elements of unfulfilled hopes and dreams attached to it, but was it really a failure by God's standard?

Martin Luther King, Jr. said, "How familiar is the experience of longing for Spain and settling for a Roman prison and how less familiar the transforming of the broken remains of a disappointed expectation into opportunities to serve God's purposes."[63] Like Paul, even if we do by chance arrive at our dreams, we find it often is not as we first envisioned. We seldom arrive as free people, but like Paul in the confinement of some unanticipated prison cell. "Written across all our lives is a fatal flaw,"[64] Dr. King Jr. declared. Paul was filled with a sense of disappointment and failure during this time in his life, and many of us understand that feeling all too well.

Paul had a deepening sense that his dreams were just outside his reach. He could touch them but not hold on to them. How do we live in a world where our utmost hopes and our expectations of God, ourselves and others are not realized? When disappointment strikes us, haunting questions surge into our minds, causing frustration, anger and depression. Philip Yancey, in his book, *Disappointment with God*, says there are three questions that haunt us in times of disappointment and apparent failure. Is God fair? Is God silent? Is God hidden? [65]

Yancey claims that the Scriptures open to us in the book of Genesis with a very interactive Creator, present as judge and king. This Creator seems to invade earth, inviting intimacy with customized punishment. Then we see Him hurt by the responses of His creation, retreating to thoughts of annihilation, a creation only to be rescued by a covenant He would make with humanity. God then steps back from humanity, it seems, and remains hidden for some time. When Moses arrives on the scene, God shows up again in full form. It is as though Moses is the Clark Kent of Egypt who can turn into Superman through the kryptonite powers of God. Punishing evil, challenging injustice, rewarding good and aggressively pursuing his purposes with people, God makes himself known. He makes himself visible in a cloud and in a pillar of fire. He reveals his power through ten plagues and the parting of the Red Sea.[65] Yet the Israelites' response to his power offers insight into the limitations of power.

Although the weight of power can touch us, it cannot change us completely. Power falls short in the most valuable arena of life; power cannot direct love. In God's case, His power did not gain the response of love. Love is exercised differently from power. His silence, therefore, may be an indicator of His love and an indicator of His unwillingness to use His power on occasions in our lives.[67] "What God cannot do through his power, he could do through his suffering,"[68] says Yancey. His commitment to die on the cross for us, although viewed as disappointment and failure, was part of an unfinished scene and bigger picture unfolding over history. What seemed as failure and insignificance required centeredness.

This is crucial for us in understanding why God puts seeds of passion and purpose within us when those very passions remain unattainable. Sometimes they remain that way for a season and sometimes for a lifetime. When we understand that our lives, when submitted to His purposes, are part of the larger drama that is unfolding over time, we begin to recognize that our part is only understood in the context of that bigger story.

Often our lives reflect only a few lines or minor parts in the larger drama, which in and of themselves seem incomplete and insignificant. Failure, to the person in pursuit of God's purpose for his or her life, is not the last word and surely not the defining issue on significance. Being secure in His love and living out our lives from the settled place as "son" or "daughter" of His is of greater weight in the matter of significance.

On the other hand, when our pursuits and passions are of our own making, like Paul's were in persecuting the first Christians, what would seem like failure can very well be success in God's eyes. It can be the tragic failures of our self-willed hearts or our negligent pursuits that cause failure to humble us and bring us to redemptive successes of our lives.

THREE BANDITS: BITTERNESS, ABANDONMENT AND FATALISM

If disappointment and apparent failure do not define our significance or measure our success in reaching for God's plan for discovering identity, passion and purpose, how do we deal with a world of unfulfilled hopes and dreams? In a western movie we often observe the good guys, while traveling on horseback or stagecoach, going through a narrow canyon only to be attacked by bandits, attempting to plunder them and their possessions. We have at least three of these bandits peering from the hills into our lives, attempting to take us off the trail of being centered along the path. In the narrow passages of disappointment and failure, we seem to be more vulnerable to their attack on our lives.

THE BANDIT OF BITTERNESS

One of our options in response to disappointment and failure is to distil our frustration into bitterness. We can harden our hearts and make them cold to God, to others and to ourselves. We can subtly begin to stop extending love; we simply become callous.[69] We can allow mistrust to rule our interactions, trusting no one and requiring trust from no one. We convince ourselves that if we expect little, it will soothe the pain of our own disappointment.

Another way to absorb bitterness into our systems is to climb to the internal summit of criticism. From that high place within we can peer, finding fault with everyone, justifying our place of mistrust. By allowing the poison of mistrust into our system it eats away at our soul's need for connection to others and we connect instead to our pain. It is natural to feel the early pangs of bitterness when we feel an injustice. But the Scriptures talk about "roots" of bitterness. *"Looking carefully lest anyone fall short of the grace of God; lest any root of bitterness springing up cause trouble, and by this many become defiled;"*[70] When we allow bitterness to stay, to fester, it takes root.

THE BANDIT OF ABANDONMENT

We can resign from life and pull inside ourselves and abandon the practice of living out life. The struggle for life ends when we give in to this bandit's attack. "We become too unconcerned to love and too passionless to hate. We become too indifferent to care and too cold to experience sorrow. We no longer smell the roses, see destiny in a sunset or hear the sound of innocence in a baby's giggle."[70] Disappointed hopes imprison us to neither life nor death. Our sentence is the confined chamber of indifference.

The bandit of bitterness pillages our emotions; the

bandit of abandonment loots our hearts while the bandit of fatalism plunders the power of our mind and will. In fatalism everything is foreordained and unavoidable.

THE BANDIT OF FATALISM

This third bandit attempts to plunder our will by weakening it through fatalism's grip. Victims often adopt an attitude of fatalism, as they do not believe they have freedom of choice, so they do not seek to be purposeful. They believe that forces beyond their control prevail over the circumstances in their life, made clear by their unwillingness to seek change. Freedom is a fable to those who stay victims; yet it is that very freedom that makes us human and allows us to have relationship with one another. By denying our freedom to choose we deny our existence as relational beings. Dr. King says, "He is, of course, right in his conviction that there is no absolute freedom and that freedom always operates within the context of predestined structure. Common experience teaches that a man is free to go north from Atlanta to Washington or south from Atlanta to Miami, but not north to Miami nor south to Washington. Freedom is always within the framework of destiny. But there is freedom." [72]

Paul became a victim and had no control over the manner in which he went to Rome or Spain, but he had control over whether he would remain a victim. Freedom gave Paul the capacity to not accept such disappointment but instead to respond, within limitations. Freedom was not a fairy tale to Paul. There was no wicked witch forcing him to remain a victim nor was there a magical glass slipper to help him escape the reality of his disappointment. It required facing his deepest fears and his experience of being victimized, by walking towards his confusion and dashed hopes, believing God would be faithful. It is the hope of

God's faithfulness that gives us the courage to grieve our losses and allow ourselves out of the prisons of denial and into the chaotic journey of anger, sorrow and release from our losses and apparent failures.

Paul turned his Roman cell into a writer's paradise as a result of the freedom to choose and freedom to trust. He looked his disappointment in the face, refusing to remain a victim, because he knew his significance was outside of that event and asked for God's wisdom and redemption. How was Paul to know that one of his expressed disappointments would become the foundation from which he would most be remembered? I am sure his prison cell kept him in a place of greater humility and greater reality as he penned his letters. How was he to know that the many letters written from the cell of disappointment would become much of the New Testament, sustaining the church for over two thousand years? When our security is in the love of God, failure can only touch us but not destroy us.

Fatalism survives on the misconception that everything good or evil is willed by God. For that reason a victim remains victimized by adopting a mindset of fatalism. Martin Luther King, Jr. said, "Although God permits evil in order to preserve the freedom of man, he does not cause evil."[73] It is outside His nature to be evil. History proves that no amount of evil, injustice or silence can squeeze out God and His capacity for redeeming evil. Yancey has told us that what God could not do through His power he could do through suffering and apparent failure. The weakness of God is stronger than the greatest strength of men.

Paul accepted that he would not fulfill his dream to preach in Spain or walk the streets of Rome as a free man. Rather than succumb to the pillaging of bandits and be left bitter, indifferent or fatalistic, he chose to see his Roman cell as a place of redemptive suffering. We must not try to escape our disappointment and failures. We need to courageously stare at our disappointments, feel their pain until we can release them and let them go. In letting go of our bitterness, abandonment and victimization we open ourselves up for God to weave his purposes in our lives through them.

In the Disney movie *"The Lion King"* we find the story of a young lion, Simba, who is pillaged by the bandits of bitterness, abandonment and fatalism in the canyons of his young life. Simba, the son of the King, Mufasa, fell victim to his Uncle's deceptive scheme. In a matter of moments, this innocent young lion cub is convinced by his uncle Scar that his own negligence has lead to his father's death. With the weight of Mufasa's death on him, Simba is chased into obscurity by his uncle's newly recruited hyena force. Simba's youthfulness left him vulnerable to be the victim. He accepted his abandonment, and allowed bitterness to take root. He then adopted the fatalism he encountered in the jungle "Hakuna Matata" as his new friends Timon and Pumbaa called it. Simba spent many years growing up in this lifestyle. While he grew older physically he remained stuck in his growth to identity, passion and purpose. He lost sight of who he was in being pillaged by bitterness, abandonment and fatalism. Eventually meeting up with a lioness and spiritual director from his past, his community called him out of his disappointment and failure. Simba had to let go of his disappointment and pain by facing it. In facing it, staring at it and then grieving it he let it go. In letting it go he placed himself back in a position to reclaim his identity, passion and purpose.

Dr. King, Jr. declared, "Almost anything that happens to us may be woven into the purposes of God. It may lengthen our cords of sympathy. It may break our self-centered pride. The cross which was willed by wicked men was woven by God into the tapestry of world redemption."[73] Those we read about earlier in Hebrews did not receive the promise of fulfilled identity, passion or purpose, yet their disappointment was not in vain. They found their significance in being centered, not in attainment. Their lives were woven into the larger picture of redemption, which only history can integrate and only faith and obedience can sustain.

DESTINED TO COMPLETION, NOT PERFECTION

While sitting in the restaurant in Vancouver looking across the table at my friends, Frank and Catherine Fabiano, I heard them ask me, "How are you doing spiritually?" About to board a plane the following day for the most exotic and exciting trip of my life, to six countries in the world, I said, "How would you be doing? I'm excited and scared, I guess."

As friends and skilled psychologists they sensed God was doing something I had not yet tapped into and asked if they could pray for me in that moment. I reached my hand awkwardly over the dinner table to their kind and loving embrace as they prayed this simple prayer, "Father, would you show Todd his need of You today?" End of prayer. I looked up at them as we ate dinner together, thankful and yet suspicious that they knew something I did not. After a long emotional and physically unsettling journey around the world, involving a panic attack and intense moments of fear, I arrived home only to be further surprised.

It was the early part of November. I was driving down to Seattle with my then three-year-old daughter Megan to speak at one of the centers of our organization. While stuck in traffic I decided to take the Advil pills I had forgotten earlier. After trying to swallow them I realized I had no water to wash them down. With an already dry mouth as a side effect, the pills lodged in my upper esophagus until they dissolved, burning through a layer of skin. As I began to feel uncomfortable and agitated I began talking out loud to God. I remember hearing my little Megan ask me, "Daddy who are you talking to?" It was a moment of innocence I needed. I eventually got out of traffic and quickly washed the Advil down with a cola. I am certain the acid did not help things.

With my throat burned, irritated and going into spasms I went to a hospital emergency to discover I had developed oesophagitis—inflammation of the esophagus. Anticipating it would heal within a week to ten days, I lived on liquids. Thirty days later I was still on liquids only to discover that my sphincter valve was not working effectively, allowing acid to come up each night and further prevent it from healing. After forty-five days of only liquids and the loss of about forty pounds, I discovered I had been brought to the end of my physical limitations. As an athletic person whose health had always been strong, I knew no physical limitations for the most part. I was disappointed with myself, my life and my inability to prevent it.

In those days my disappointment along with my inability to will myself through it scared me and unnerved me. I had to come to the end of myself in certain ways and saw that I was getting some significance in perfection or my ability to perform. It was in being broken physically and emotionally that I recognized that I could find significance in disappointment.

During those four to six months, I could hardly function as a father and a husband and a leader. I had turned over all the day-to-day leadership of the organization to others, as I did not have the emotional strength to carry things. I had wanted perfection, but God wanted me to understand it was about completion. It was about who I would become, not what I would do. My failure in not being able to function in the tasks of husband, father and a leader added further disappointment to me.

Yet that disappointment actually became the raw materials for what God was doing in me, further completion of His love in me. It was another crossroads for my life. It proved to be a landmark experience for redefining significance in my life. Facing my disappointment in not being able to perform allowed me to experience more of the grief that was deep inside. Releasing more of that grief served as a catalyst in helping me exchange a journey of perfection for a journey towards completion. I was becoming.

I had reached two unanticipated desires; greater trust in God and greater awareness of my frailty as a human. I now could trust God at a deeper level when I could not trust myself or protect myself. I had allowed God to father me in areas I did not entrust to Him before. I was less perfect yet more complete, becoming more like Christ on the inside. Failure and unfulfilled dreams do not carry the final say for our reward of obedience.

The journey towards completion is the journey of becoming. We are never complete, but it is the journey that matters, not the goal of attaining something tangible. Identity, passion and purpose are formed in journeying to completion, not perfection. Staying secure in the love of Christ and not giving way to disappointment and failure allows us to "become" like Him. Granted, it takes more strength and courage to continue on the road of obedience in the middle of disappointment and failure than in the middle of attainment, yet the reward is the same—actually, the reward is greater.

FINDING MEANING IN UNFULFILLED HOPES AND DREAMS

The culmination of Paul's dream to go to Rome and then on into Spain reached a defining moment in Acts chapter twenty-one. Paul, while returning from a missionary journey, stopped in Caesarea at the home of Phillip the evangelist. With anticipation, his friends awaited their cherished guest and friend, Paul. When he finally did arrive, he stayed with them for several days.

One evening after sharing a meal together, Paul began to tell them stories of his journeys. All eyes were fastened on him as he captivated his Caesarean audience with stories of God's providence. All the while a familiar but unexpected guest from Jerusalem arrived at their door. Greeted by his hosts, this tall bearded man, whose frame filled the doorway, seemed insensitive to their welcoming. He invited himself into this moment with a focused yet calm demeanor. While Paul was in mid sentence, Agabus entered the room, changing the atmosphere. Many knew who he was though they had never met him.

Paul gave way to Agabus' presence, stopping his thought to acknowledge this unexpected guest. Agabus, knowing that he had been given this moment, reached over and took a belt from the chair beside him and in a dramatic fashion carried out his mission. As he looked past everyone, as though he was reading thoughts from somewhere in his mind's eye, he began to wrap the belt around his ankles, binding them together. Taking the end he began to wrap his wrists together with the remainder of the belt. As his final wrap completed he uttered these words *"The Holy Spirit declares, so shall the owner of this belt be bound by Jewish leaders in Jerusalem and turned over to the Romans."*[75]

In that moment all eyes in the room shifted immediately to Paul, as they all knew he was the owner. All those present begged Paul not to carry on with his plans to go to Jerusalem as they felt it was God's warning of protection. Paul was prepared for this moment. He responded to his friends and co-workers by asking them not to make this more difficult for him by weeping for him. He had realized some time ago that this might be his fate and had already looked his hopes of going to Rome as a free man straight in the eyes and concluded *"he was not only willing to be jailed but die for the sake of the Lord Jesus."*[76]

When Paul could not be persuaded they released him and together trusted God. Paul eventually arrived at Rome in chains, as Agabus had predicted, not as Paul had originally hoped. Paul knew even death, the greatest experience of finality to disappointment, does not determine significance. So Paul accepted the belt from Agabus that day, a symbol of unfulfilled dreams and hopes, and was marched to his Roman cell, never to walk the streets of Spain. Paul eventually found meaning in that Roman cell but not until he had accepted his disappointment.

Dr. King said it so potently, "The Christian faith makes it possible for us nobly to accept that which cannot be changed, to meet disappointments and sorrow with an inner poise, and to absorb the most intense pain without abandoning our sense of hope, for we know as Paul testified, in life and in death, in Spain and in Rome 'that all things work together for good to them that love God, to them who are the called according to his purpose.'"[77]

DAVID'S STORY

King David, whose story of disappointment and failure has been passed from generation to generation, reminds us of the power of God to turn all things together for good and according to His purposes for our lives. David, out of the moral will of God in his adulterous relationship with Bathsheba, found meaning in his failure. David's first son born to Bathsheba died, leaving them to mourn the child's death and their loss.

Yet God's purposes emerged even out of David's pain and failure. Solomon was the second son born to David and

Bathsheba. Solomon not only grew up to be the wisest man to ever walk the earth, the Scriptures claim, but became the son that inherited his father's throne, grafting him into the lineage of Christ.

David's acceptance of his failure and grief over the disappointment actually made way for God to weave meaning into David's apparent failures. Finding meaning and significance in unfulfilled dreams and hopes begin by acknowledging and grieving disappointment and failure and by staying centered in the love of God. Staying centered involves the constant struggle of fighting our way back to honesty and transparency in our relationship with God and others.

The journey of discovering identity, passion and purpose often involves a voyage through disappointment and failure. That voyage involves staving off the bandits of bitterness, withdrawal and fatalism, which try to take us off course. It also means we recognize that God is most interested in our completion in His love. His seed of love that has been planted within us—not our perfection—is His highest concern. As each generation pursues this journey, each generation needs its own personal experience of knowing meaning in disappointment and failure. If we do not understand that significance and failure are separated, we will avoid the necessary risks which will later be the raw materials by which we discover a purer identity, passion and purpose.

Chapter 5
Process Questions

1. What obstacles of disappointment and failure have affected your identity, passions and purpose?

2. Have you been attacked by any of the three bandits (bitterness, abandonment, fatalism)? If so how have you responded?

3. How have you allowed those "bandits" to thwart the purposes of God for your life?

4. In what ways are you being made complete in God's love?

5. What meaning have you discovered in disappointment and failure?

6. If you are stuck in areas of disappointment and failure can you see a way out?

CHAPTER 6
IN OUR INSIGNIFICANCE
WE ARE CHOSEN

SOMETHING DAVIDIC ABOUT US ALL

I heard the phone ring but thought nothing of it until Maryanne yelled my name from across the room in our North Vancouver apartment. "What is the matter?" I said to her.

"You won't believe who is on the phone," she replied.

"Who is it then?" I anxiously inquired.

"An adoption reunion agency," she said.

"What?" I said.

"My birth mother is looking for me and wants to meet me," she replied.

"What if she is a bag lady in downtown Vancouver looking for help after all these years?" I responded.

"Quiet, I am trying to listen," she instantly responded, as though she had not heard my rude comment. Hanging up the phone she turned to me and said, "I think I should meet her, at least to say thank you."

At twenty-eight years of age Maryanne was content, and had been throughout her life. She never really had entertained the idea of searching for her birth mother. When this landed in her lap, her only thought was to meet her and thank her for her unselfishness by wanting what was best for her. She agreed on the phone that we would meet. She immediately called her mom and dad to tell them of the unpredicted events that transpired that day.

Within forty-eight hours, we met her birth mother, along with her birth father. We discovered that her birth mother, who was sixteen at the time of her birth, had contact with her for three days, letting her know she loved her and that her decision to give her away was best for Maryanne. Four years later, her birth mother married her birth father and together had two more girls, Kelsey and Julie. Maryanne had been adopted at eight days old by her mom and dad and had known little of the details surrounding her birth and her birth mother. All she had ever been told was that her birth mother was fifteen years old when she had her at Grace Hospital in Vancouver.

What has constantly surprised me about Maryanne over the seventeen years I have known her, fourteen of which we have been married, is how secure she is in knowing she is loved. Some who have been adopted question their significance, because they were not kept. I have come to realize otherwise about Maryanne. Though the process of adoption may substantiate feelings of insignificance for some, she has always known she was loved and chosen. While the scars of rejection can mark many adopted children, it was the realization that she had been chosen that marked her. If I know one thing about Maryanne and if she knows one thing about life, it is this: her dad loves her. Her mom and dad, unable to have children eventually chose to adopt. Jeff, her older brother, was first adopted and then Maryanne, only for her parents to later conceive twin girls, Wendy and Laura.

Her childhood needs were provided for by a loving and nurturing home. Her memories are that of being the apple of her father's eye. Watching the two of them interact over the years, I have come to agree. His unconditional acceptance and embrace of her is apparent and immovable. Though the events surrounding her birth could have sown seeds of rejection in her life, the loving embrace of her mother and father allowed the real truth of her life to be known: in what appeared as insignificance, she was chosen. Maryanne's life is a reflection of what all our lives are destined towards.

Being adopted is the primary relationship all Christians hold with their Heavenly Father. *"His unchanging plan has always been to adopt us into his own family by bringing us to himself through Jesus Christ. And this gave him great pleasure."*[78] When we begin to recognize that in "my insignificance I am chosen"[79] we begin to understand how identity, passion and purpose are to be lived out. It is not our greatness, giftedness, passionate embrace of life or even our uniqueness that ultimately makes a place for us in the world. It is the profound truth that despite the seeds of insignificance in all of us, we have found favor with God. It is not we who make ourselves significant, it is the identity of the one who chooses us that ultimately defines our significance.

Saul was King of Israel. He was Israel's first King. Samuel the prophet was authorized by God to pronounce Saul king. As a man who stood above the crowd, Saul defeated armies, mobilized people and won the hearts of many in Israel. At one point in the Saul story we are invited into a dialogue between God and Samuel over the grief of Saul's leadership. God seemed to be indicating to Samuel that He was sorry that He had ever made Saul King, *"for he has not been loyal to me and has refused to obey me"*[80] and as a result was inviting Samuel to enact another plan not yet revealed to Saul. The Lord told Samuel to go to Bethlehem and find a man named Jesse. Samuel was instructed on his arrival to invite Jesse and his sons to join him and at that time God would show him which one of Jesse's sons would be the next King. Beginning with the eldest, Jesse brought his seven sons into the presence of this seasoned prophet.

As Eliab, the eldest and most handsome of Jesse's sons moved towards Samuel his stature alone commanded attention. He walked like a first-born, confident, bold and sure of his place. He stood out like Saul did. I am sure

Samuel muttered under his breath, 'This will be easy; it is obviously him.'

Yet the Lord interrupted Samuel, as though he heard his thoughts and said to Samuel, *"Don't judge by appearance or height, for I have rejected him. The Lord doesn't make decisions the way you do."*[81] Then Abinadad was brought before Samuel only to be disappointed. Then Shammah, the third eldest, until all seven had passed by Samuel. I am sure as that seventh son passed by Samuel, he questioned his discernment. Have I got the right city, the right Jesse?

With Jesse now embarrassed and Samuel confused, they stared at one another in silence. Finally Samuel broke the silence by interjecting a question. *"Are these all the sons you have?"*[82] He asked with hesitation in his voice.

Jesse replied, *"There is still the youngest, but he is not even in Bethlehem."*[83] I am sure by now Jesse's embarrassment had turned to humiliation, as he had not thought to mention his youngest son to Samuel. The Hebrew word here used for *youngest* has undertones of insignificance or not counting for much, which is an indicator of why Jesse did not consider his youngest as a prime candidate.[84]

It is here in the Scriptures that we meet David for the first time—a young, innocent and insignificant boy as far as his family was concerned. After having been left out of the family gathering to stay and tend the sheep, David arrived in Bethlehem to meet the look of contempt in his older brothers and the look of surprise in his father. Samuel looked into the face of this ruddy and handsome young man and said, *"This is the one; annoint him."*[85]

David, not fully aware of what was happening, happily received God's blessing on his life. He was chosen not for what his brothers or his father saw in him but for what God saw in him. This is how we are introduced to the David Story. Eugene Peterson calls the David story "The most extensively narrated single story in this larger story [of scripture]."[86] The David story touches the widest range of human experience inviting us to observe "as a person comes alive before God—aware of God, responsive to God,"[87] The central account of what it means to live by faith in the Scriptures comes to us not on the back of a white horse or in the center of a gold platter but in the form of David, an ordinary person.

The storyteller of First Samuel skillfully crafted his intention in the David story. The storyteller, God, communicates to the reader that "there is something Davidic about us all; that in our insignificance we are chosen," as Peterson writes. The choice of David—the runt, the shepherd, the forgotten one—has a clear and poignant message for us all. We have found favor with God not because of our greatness but because of His greatness.

"We are not complete and we are not fully human," claims Peterson. When we are fully human our incompleteness is evidenced all around us and "all around our incompletion is God."[88] When we embrace our humanity we embrace our ordinariness. Only when we embrace our ordinariness can we fully recognize the profound impact of God's choice and favor in choosing us.

The David story is that story and the God-story He desires for all our lives. God is the hero in David's story, not David. When we become fully human then and only then can we recognize that it is God we need. David's life invites us each day to again accept God's choice of us. He invites us to be His choice while we are still mired in our insignificance and inadequacies. It is in the incompleteness of being fully human that the God-story of our lives can be found. It is in that story that we recognize His favor, calling out the Davidic nature in us all. It is that kind of underserved favor we receive which enables us to walk with humility and serve others. Discovering our identity, passion and purpose is recognizing this profound favor and the implications of that favor; in our insignificance we have been chosen.

SERVING IS AT THE HEART OF BEING CHOSEN

When we know we are chosen, when we know we are favored, our security is settled. When we know we are favored, competition evaporates from the equation of our everyday lives. Favor is not on a teeter-totter like reality in our relationships, where one must be down for another to be up. Our significance does not require the insignificance of another to substantiate it. God has always been the God of the many. Although it is through the few that we learn of Him, He has always reached for the many. God's invitation has at all times been to all but often only responded to by the few, potentially making His favor seem withheld. Favor is extended to all who will receive it, the Scriptures clearly teach.

The requirement is to first embrace our humanity, which results in embracing our incompleteness. At the heart of discovering our identity, passion and purpose is this heart, knowing we are chosen and favored. We should not approach our lives as though we are pirates on a mission to loot some stolen treasure or be the first to find hidden treasure lost by others. There is enough treasure for all and favor received cannot be taken from us.

Discovering who we are, our God-given passions and our undiscovered purpose for our individual lives is not about us at the core; it is about others. It is discovering "otherness" that is at the center of this journey. The pursuit and eventual laying hold of our identity, passion and purpose are intended for serving others.

Here is the paradox: we seek to find so we can give away. We do not discover identity, passion and purpose simply for our own benefit but for the sake of others.

Christianity has always been about the other and to be truly Christian one must travel the road to otherness. Otherness involves bringing delight to God and being aware of others. In order to reach otherness we must discover ourselves, we must know ourselves and we must share ourselves. When we are authentic we are able to touch others because our incompleteness, which is always a mixture of our growth and our brokenness, can then be touched. Presenting anything more is scandalous while presenting anything less exposes our inability to apprehend a servant's heart.

We stood on the streets of Ottawa, Ontario; amazed at the reception we were being given. It was noon time and people were shuffling from place to place, focused on their destination yet honestly distracted by us. Was it us, our music or something more profound than we knew that was attracting them? We had come together only eight days earlier having gathered youth from across Canada to participate in presenting choreographed movement and song at a large assembly of Christian leaders in Ottawa.

We had hand picked a group of youth to represent Canada, with whom we spent five days preparing. We were amazed at the responses we had received along the way. Favor was all around us it seemed. In the convention of over a thousand pastors, on the streets, everywhere we went, we were wholeheartedly received.

While riding on this high, we landed at our final destination, a soup kitchen in downtown Ottawa. It was the end of several long days and our team was exhausted. Often in those times we can be ripe for experiencing our own reality. In our preparation we spent time examining the condition of our hearts spiritually as our goal was not to perform, but to be vulnerable and authentic in sharing our gifts of music and movement through our incompleteness.

We seemed rushed that day in our preparation and unusually hurried to commence. In a scrambled mode we landed in the presence of over two hundred hungry men awaiting a meal. The soup kitchen that we found ourselves in required each person to listen for thirty minutes to a presentation or talk in order to receive a free meal.

As the ritual began you knew that these men's minds were not on our presentation but on their stomachs. They were in need of food and we were a means to that end. We were on a journey discovering our identity, passion and purpose, yet had barely touched the reality of otherness. They were on a journey to discovering their hunger, thirst and sleep destination that night and had barely touched the reality of their need of acceptance.

We were unprepared, rattled, and in need of some humility, while they were distracted, disinterested and in need of something real. It would either prove to be a dynamic recipe for change or a recipe for disaster, depending on our willingness to be transparent to be vulnerable, to be authentic, to reach them.

About half way through the music of our first song the background tape, for no apparent reason, tightened in the tape player, resulting in the music moving up an entire octave. The vocalists were further rattled as they desperately tried to find the notes and get back on key. As the song came to a close, their voices found the key giving relief for only a brief moment. Prior to the second song one of the fourteen-year-old Korean girls came up to say something into the microphone. We had entrusted to the team the privilege of coming and sharing at any given time if they felt they had something to say.

No amount of training could have prepared me for what she was about to do and say. Her words were raw and real, "I can't do this anymore!" She had my attention and our distracted audience's attention for a moment. She then said, "I am upset with my sister and I did not deal with it before we came to share and I am sorry." As she began to cry, she was embraced by her sister who came out of the back row of our team to hold her. They stood there together weeping; seemingly unaware as a partially interested but still distracted audience looked on.

Eventually this intimate moment ended and the next song started, much to my relief. By about the third song there was hardly a dry eye on our team's face. They were flustered and the reality of their inability to penetrate their captive audience pushed back on them, moving them to tears. They were confronted with the reality of otherness or lack of it. Up until then their service cost them little emotionally as they had never been rejected. Were they to sing to be received or sing to serve no matter the reception? Could they know favor enough to just sing to God alone whether they were received or not by people?

By about the middle of our presentation there was a turning point moving them down the road to otherness. Mark, one of our young men, reached over to grasp the microphone. I hesitated inside, as I had no idea what he might do. He was our *team clown* who had rarely said a serious thing, and at a time like this he was not my first pick for a communicator. As a fifteen-year-old, he stood there in front of these seemingly disinterested men with his head bowed to the ground. It seemed like forever, yet I imagine it was only minutes. Finally as Mark looked up I saw only tears pouring down his cheeks. I was struck by his countenance as I listened to him, touched by the experience of otherness, which he allowed to be expressed in a most vulnerable way.

As he looked into the faces of these broken and impoverished men he said this, "For the first time in my life I have felt God's heart for someone and I feel his heart for you." His shoulders and head slumped forward as he continued to weep in their presence. Eventually he put the microphone down and walked back to join his team as they continued to share their choreographed music.

After the final song I had anticipated a mass exodus because the thirty minutes was completed and dinner was being served. Instead they remained seated, soaking it all in, but one would not know it from their appearance. Though they seemed distant and cold on the outside, the honesty of these youth warmed and softened them on the inside. We had invited them to stay for personal prayer. For as much as thirty minutes many of them stayed to receive prayer.

As I walked towards one man he said words to me that I will never forget, as they defined that experience: "There are three things in the world that are the same, you know," he said in a matter of fact way.

I curiously replied, "Oh really, what are they?"

He quickly responded "Dogs, kids and street people."

"And how is that?" I said with interest.

Leaning forward he whispered, "We can all tell a phony." Then his guard came down and he said with softened eyes, "I have been coming here for fifteen years and this is the purest thing I have ever seen in my life. Will you pray for me?" I was so shaken by his words I could hardly focus on praying for him. Here I am, awkwardly enduring the level of intimacy that is being expressed, wanting to apologize for these young people and yet this man is finally seeing something real.

As these young people were on a journey to discover what it means to serve, they were confronted with their lack of otherness. They understood that discovering otherness costs you something—the commitment to be transparent and vulnerable. These men on the journey to discover a reason to live another day were touched by something, something that could reach them, something incomplete yet real. These youth could not have served those men that day who had heard it all, unless they expressed authentic humanity. These young people experienced a servant's heart that day, exposing them to a deeper level of otherness and the requirement for it.

David, described as *"a man after [God's] own heart"*[89] was put on the road to otherness at an early stage. Bringing delight to God and becoming aware of others was worked into David's life in a most challenging way. After being chosen, David had to face mixed messages sent to him by the king he was called to serve. Embrace and withdrawal, endearment and rejection, tenderness and hardness were all confusing messages sent to David by King Saul on a regular basis. David was called to serve a jealous, hardened and, at times, insane king. He was called to serve when he would not be received and called to serve when his life was in grave danger.

David spent most of his twenties on the run, living in the wilderness, far from his calling and far from completion. David, faced with his incompleteness, learned to serve with a heart of transparency and vulnerability. He learned to be real and to accept his humanity. In accepting his humanity he opened himself to God's sovereignty. It was later said of David that he *"shepherded them with integrity of heart; with skillful hands he led them."*[90] David's journey to otherness, though unanticipated, embedded in him the central ingredient for his identity, passion and purpose—a servant's heart. David found security in God in his wilderness years thereby making him effective in serving others.

Jesus modeled for us service with complete security. *"Jesus knew that the Father had put all things under his power, and that he had come from God and was returning to God; so he got up from the meal, took off his outer clothing and wrapped a towel around his waist. After that, he poured water into a basin and began to wash his disciples' feet, drying them with a towel that was wrapped around him."*[91] Jesus knew who He was and where He was going. His identity, passion and purpose were secured; therefore He could enter otherness completely.

The depth of our security reflects the depth of our ability to serve another with the discovery of our identity, passion and purpose. Once we discover them we can let them go because we know we are chosen and favored. We do not have to defend ourselves or manipulate outcomes; we are free to serve.

The discovery of identity, passion and purpose is not about self-improvement or self-actualization; rather it is about delighting God and becoming aware of others. It is about finding something so we can give it away. Jesus could get down on His knees and wash His disciple's feet because He knew He was chosen and did not need to protect who He was, His passions or His purpose. He did not have to defend his passions, prove His identity or convince others of His purpose. When we see life in this way our service comes from a secure place, as did Jesus'. Until then our journey to discover identity, passion and purpose is so much about us, which is self-centered, not God-centered. Gaining a servant's heart is at the center of this journey.

SELLING OUT TO YOUR IDENTITY, PASSION AND PURPOSE

"Don't be ridiculous!" Saul replied. "There is no way you can go against this Philistine. You are only a boy, and he has been in the army since he was a boy!"

But David persisted. "I have been taking care of my father's sheep," he said. "When a lion or a bear comes to steal a lamb from the flock, I go after it with a club and take the lamb from its mouth. If the animal turns on me, I catch it by the jaw and club it to death. I have done this to both lions and bears, and I will do it to this pagan Philistine, too, for he has defied the armies of the living God! The Lord who saved me from the lion and bear will save me from this Philistine."[92]

David remembered as a young teenage boy how he had stood at the back entrance of his home, his clothes torn as blood dripped down his side from the gouges his body displayed at the hands of the lion that turned on him. He stood there with a tuft of the lion's mane tightly grasped in his hand as his look of wonder said it all. His body, though oozing blood and pain, was oozing something even more vital—fulfillment and faith.

David, while shepherding the sheep entrusted to him, was faced with the cost of the position given to him. Would he give himself for the sheep? David in this story had taken his first steps toward otherness and toward selling out to his identity, passion and purpose. David, faced with the cost of attacking the lion and bear to defend the sheep, was faced with selling out to his call.

It is one thing to know something; it is quite another to give yourself to what you know. We can know who we are, our passions and purpose, and yet never serve others because we do not sell out in an attempt to keep our options open. David was faced with many steps of faith along his journey. Each step of faith that David took further settled who he was, what he was about and what he would give his life for.

Our lives are defined and marked by the times when we sell out to what we know. Those times are transition times of growth and often come when the stakes are high, the cost is great and the road is narrow or unknown. They require faith and a step of faith. It is otherness—the delight of God and awareness of others that will often propel us through those times.

David had not anticipated the most transitional day of his life, the day he would unknowingly sell out to his purpose. David, as a college-age student, was going back and forth between serving King Saul and serving his father in Bethlehem. While with his father he was asked to take rations to his brothers who were battling on the front lines of the war with the Philistines.

As David arrived on the scene, the Philistine giant, Goliath, had been taunting the Israelites for forty days by challenging them to choose someone to fight him. As David delivered his rations he watched Goliath step out of the Philistine ranks to shout his challenge. As David heard it, something began stirring in him. He asked, *"Who is this pagan Philistine anyway, that he is allowed to defy the armies of the living God?"*[93]

David was feeling a faith beginning to rise within him calling him to step forward into his identity, passion and purpose. However it would cost him something. The stakes were high and the risks real. David also had to risk his relationship with Saul, as Saul was not convinced that David was up for the task, either.

In that moment David had to give release to his faith or his identity, passion and purpose would have been delayed until faith was released in a later opportunity. David that day began his journey to otherness by selling out to God's call. He did not think of himself or of his best interests but instead on the impact this would have on his people, his family, and his nation. David was thinking like the king he was to become.

We had arrived that night in the city of Bergama in Western Turkey or what was referred to as Pergamum in the Scriptures. There were almost twenty of us, including my wife Maryanne and our sixteen-month-old daughter Megan, who had taken this trek down the western shores of Turkey. We were in search of the ancient city Pergamum at this point in the journey and more specifically the coliseum where the early Christian martyrs were thrown to the lions. Western Turkey, formerly known as Asia Minor contained some of the cities written to in the New Testament including Ephesus and Colosse. We wanted to see and pray at some of the ancient landmarks that formed early Christianity, yet knowing Turkey was a Muslim country today.

Jeremy, one of our team members who was about thirteen years old, came to me the first morning we were there to tell me of a dream he had had the night before. He said in his dream that a lion was chasing him through his school hallways back in New Brunswick when the scene changed to ancient times. As the lion chased him, he had three weapons in the dream: a sword, a gun and a bow and arrow to fight the lion. He was excited to tell me that after the lion chased him for some time in the dream, he eventually killed it.

At first I dismissed it as a boy's dream. Jeremy then said to me, "Don't you get it?"

I said, "Get what?"

"This dream is for here and now," he said assuredly.

I said "Oh, really."

Jeremy began to tell me that he had this dream before, in fact several times over the years. However he had never killed the lion in the dream until that night. Now he had my attention. I am not given to dreams much but I did understand that there was something to this boy's dream.

As we found our way to the coliseum, which was off the beaten track, we could see the ancient landmark protruding from the hardened soil. An older sunken arch remained while the grass grown over the stadium left ridges down the bowl like steps. A creek flowed through the bottom into the remains of the rock caverns that once held the fierce lions. Standing in the bottom we could imagine the twenty four thousand onlookers engaged in the drama of lion feeding. Pink flowering trees grew out of the creek bank below, reminding me that life comes out of death.

We wandered and soaked in the environment for some

time before we gathered to pray. As we were about to pray Jeremy turned to me and said "This is the place!"

"What place?" I said.

"I know how we are to pray," he said.

"Okay, Jeremy, go for it then," I replied.

Jeremy began to tell us that he had three weapons in his dream and that he felt those weapons were indicators of how we were to pray here for the people of Turkey. The sword, which was God's word, the gun, which was the name of Jesus and the bow and arrow, which was our worship, defined for him the direction of our prayers:

We first begin to just pray out Scriptures from the Bible that came to us as we waited quietly. After several Scriptures were prayed, my sister Tracey felt she should read and pray the story of the stoning of Stephen in the Book of Acts, describing the story of the first martyr for Christ. We were all emotional as we were being impacted by the reality of standing in this coliseum alone, waiting for the lion's pounce to take one's life for one's faith.

Later on we stood together and began to say the name of Jesus out loud, asking Him to bring His presence to this land again. Then we ended over an hour later by singing songs of worship. After singing a few songs I began to hear the sounds of something flying past me ending in loud thumps on the ground. This continued and multiplied as the sound increased. I looked up and to my surprise there above us stood ten to twenty Turkish children hurling rocks at us with hatred in their faces. Earlier these children, whose language we could not speak, hung around us smiling as we smiled in return. They seemed unhindered by our presence until we worshipped.

Our team, full of faith and spirituality, began to reach down to pick up rocks to return the favor. I said, "Wait a minute; something important is happening. Let's not retaliate." We stood there as rocks hurled by us in increasing numbers. Only one rock had struck a team member. The feelings of vulnerability were real though, and the cost of our prayers was becoming real. It was one thing to know something and it was quite another to give ourselves to what we knew. We had the choice to sell out to our prayers now and we did faithfully.

After about fifteen minutes of experiencing these children's attempt to stone us, we sensed that we could walk away now. We had allowed ourselves to experience at a deeper level the cost of Christianity. We slowly turned and walked out of the ancient ruins, our hearts beating quickly, and somewhat shaken while the awareness of giving ourselves in such a dramatic way to prayer settled into us. Our Turkish bus driver had been yelling across the coliseum to the children only to be included in the assault.

As we arrived at our hotel that evening, I received a message from the mayor of Bergmam, apologizing for the events of our day. Because I knew it was spiritual in nature, I had hoped he would not to be too hard on the kids. We had faced that day with whether we would sell out to our purpose and prayers. Our presence and prayers unearthed the spiritual residue from some two thousand years earlier and we were faced with that reality. We were tested with what we knew and whether we would give ourselves to it or just talk about what we believed.

Jeremy's dream and subsequent willingness to sell out allowed us all to experience with him that in our insignificance we were chosen. That ancient coliseum served the purpose of allowing us to take little steps of faith that day, giving us strength for greater steps of faith ahead in each of our lives.

FAITHFUL BEFORE SUCCESSFUL

True life as opposed to mere existence is measured by the quality of our relationships—the otherness of our lives.

While we need to sell out to the purposes of God that come our way we must remember that the goal is otherness, bringing delight to God and becoming aware of others.

Otherness, when it grows into maturity forms into community. To the degree that we experience the essence of community, which is belonging, openness and connectedness is to the degree we experience true life. True life then is defined by the quality of our existence not the achievement of goals.

Although we pursue goals, we realize it is the process that brings meaning, not goal-achievement. This processing involves interaction with people, and people make up community. Being chosen for otherness allows us to be free to be faithful in our journey not necessarily being successful in attaining a specific goal.

Many of us are not sure how to measure our lives because we are taught to measure it by our accomplishments or achievements, when in reality it is only our relationships that are eternal. On our journey to identity, passion and purpose, the otherness of our lives will often require faithfulness of us with no assurance of success. Without recognizing this reality, community often becomes a means to an end, and we trample over relationships in the process to discover who we are, what we are about and what we should give our lives for, when in reality those relationships were the end.

I have been guilty of this in my journey. Not recognizing that otherness takes priority over forging identity, passion and purpose in my life has caused me to squander some treasured relationships. My brother, Dean, has been a most potent reminder in my life of this journey to relationship. Although he and I are very different, we actually complete each other well, yet I could rarely see that. For starters, when growing up, I was the older brother who was frustrated by his lack of care for our environment. Rather than realizing he was the more sensitive one—carrying the emotions for our family at times—I punished him emotionally for being so unmotivated.

In family systems theory, various members of the family carry emotions or behavior that reflects the health of the whole system. Families are seen as interconnected emotional systems that require balance for the system to exist. Often there are members of any given family system who carry the unhealthy aspects of the whole family. They reflect or demonstrate the unhealthy aspects of the whole system, not just their own condition.

My brother often carried that role in our family, but rather than accept that or understand that, I at times walked over him in my journey to discovery, unaware he was reflecting some of my sickness. There have been windows along the way in our relationship where I have seen the treasure and beauty of who he is, but they often got lost in my pursuit of success.

Coming to the end of me, on the trip around the world, which started my six-month illness that I talked about earlier in this book, proved to be the best thing to shape me towards seeing otherness as the end goal. It caused me to face the deep grief, losses and unresolved pain that was driving me and had made me an adrenalin addict. Since that time I have been on the journey of understanding my identity, passion and purpose in the context of otherness. It has been an increasing journey of preferring others, recognizing that the goal is relationship and that the treasure is found in community. For a rugged individualist, a survivor of traumatic events, this has been a hard and painful journey. Now that I know so little and have a grasp on even less, I realize my need for God and others.

Faithfulness in relationships has been making its way to the front row of my life over the last nine years. As a result, I am slowly realizing that eternity is all about people, not accomplishments. In recent times I have been finding new freedoms in my relationship with my brother. He has changed, but more importantly I have changed and I recognize his value and who we are together in more sustained ways.

CHOSEN FOR COMMUNITY

We can come to the place of recognizing that our story is God's story, as did David, and that in our insignificance, we too are chosen. We have been chosen for otherness and when otherness is increasingly expressed, community can be formed. The experience of community shapes and completes the process of our journey toward identity, passion and purpose because it is cyclical. The journey to the discovery of identity, passion and purpose necessitates community and further results in community. Without community we will by no means fully reach our discovery of identity, passion and purpose and yet when we experience it, deeper and wider community results.

It is within community with God and others that we discover ourselves, discover otherness and connect at levels of intimacy reserved only for humans. For a human being to define him or herself, yet be unknown to others seems a mystery at best, but is most likely untruth. It is in community that we become known and it is in being known that our life takes shape. Community requires of us dependency, vulnerability and humility, yet leaves us connected, protected and fulfilled when that community starts with God as the center.

T.H White in his book "*The Sword and Stone*" portrays the creation story in a most surreal manner. Though his tale is not meant to portray the facts of the creation story, it clearly captures one aspect of the creation story: our humanity. It defines our design as vulnerable and dependent, making us prime candidates for community. In White's book we read that on the final day of creation God brought all the embryos before him. God had created all the species in embryo form, actually the same form. The form of each embryo looked helplessly human. Each of the embryos had their arms that hung unprotected from their shoulders, their exposed body and their defenseless legs that feebly hung from their frame. They had no shield from the elements and not many tools within their design to help them defend themselves or to provide for themselves. As God lined up all the embryos before Him, He gave them their options. He let them know that each species of embryo could trade in parts of their frail and unprotected designs for armor and weapons but only up to three trades each. For example, one could trade in his arms for wings to help him fly or his legs for webbed paddles to aid him in swimming. They could trade in their unprotected skin for feathers or fur, their tender hands for claws and digging instruments or their mouths for weapon-like teeth and jaws. However, God said to each embryo that whatever it chose would be its unchanging state for eternity so He challenged them to choose wisely.

As each species conferred together, one by one they came up with a plan. Some traded in their arms for wings, others for weapons. Some traded in their skin for fur, others for feathers. Some gained long narrow beaks, while others chose wide and powerful jaws. Some chose claws on all their appendages while others on only two. Some chose to add a tail while others added hair. As God came to the final species, human kind, he looked down upon them and said, "O, little man what is your decision?"

The little embryo said to God, "This is how I see it. O, God, you seem to know best what you were doing in making our design. Instead of trading in our hands for tools we will make tools, and instead of trading in our legs for paddles we will build boats. Instead of trading in our unprotected bodies for fur or feathers we will wear some protection. We think you knew what you were doing, so we choose to stay in this vulnerable place, dependent."

God looked down on the little embryo with a smile as he turned to the other embryos. "As for the rest of you embryos from this day forward you will remain forever unchanging and instinct with rule you." Then he turned to mankind and said, "As for you, little man, you have chosen well. From this day forward you will rule the fish of the sea and birds of the air and the creatures on land. You will remain potential, able to change and grow yet forever dependent, for you have chosen me as your protector." [94]

In this tale we see the vulnerability of our humanity exposed. "Love is what we most want, yet it is what we fear the most. Love makes us vulnerable and open, but then we can be hurt through rejection and separation,"[95] says Jean Vanier. Unlike other creatures we have little instinct. We are made dependent and in need of others' love and in need of God's love daily. We are not unchanging or static but have the capacity for relationship, love and growth. Simply said, when we remain dependent on God and others, community can help shape us. Identity, passion and purpose are not static elements of community either. They are instead, dynamic processes of our lives that are growing, changing and ever shaping us as we love and grow and live in relationship with God and others.

The journey spoken of throughout White's book can begin in each of us when we recognize we are made helplessly human. The place of greatest privilege and purpose in creation requires the place of greatest dependency and vulnerability, and that is what we are called to. Humility allows us to embrace our humanity and in embracing our humanity we come to the realization that in our insignificance we have been chosen. This humility gives us eyes to see wisdom in those who have gone before us while giving us vision to lend a hand to those coming behind us. In this intergenerational cord of humanity, we find the vision and sustaining power for passing on identity, passion and purpose. We have been chosen for community.

Chapter 6
Process Questions

1. What opportunities have you accepted in serving others with your passions and purpose?

2. What small steps of faith have you taken towards your passions and purpose?

3. When circumstances have presented you with the opportunity to "sell out" to your identity, passion and purpose. Did you take them? If not why?

4. How have you allowed yourself to be vulnerable regarding your passions and purpose?

5. Do you recognize when you bring delight to God's heart day to day?

6. How have you understood "otherness" in your journey of living life?

CHAPTER 7
THE INVITATION OF COMMUNITY

A FRACTURED HUMANITY

Although each of us has an unfolding story, we relate to a common story that binds us together and makes us distinctively human. The emergence of our life on this planet, though innocent and untainted in appearance, often leaves our true identities unclaimed, our passions unfulfilled, and our sense of purpose betrayed as our life marches toward completion.

Our entrance into this life is often marked by the sentiment of homelessness and fatherlessness on the inside. Homelessness is an uncertainty in our hearts with regard to our place and belonging in the world. Fatherlessness, on the other hand, is a deeper sense of not knowing who we are, where we fit and why we are here. Time and again we experience the overwhelming sense of our fatherlessness through our insecurities. This uncertainty is often connected to the question of our existence. We are searching for something on the inside that feels like home, something to complete us. We are searching for a place where we feel accepted and can thrive, a place called home. As a result our lives become a journey to complete ourselves.

In this search, some exchange these greater longings for lesser ones. Others become fugitives from themselves hoping to escape the completion that they do not possess, and still others exist completely unaware that a search is in progress, living life without asking the deeper questions. We take on socially acceptable searches: a marriage or a career to complete us, or dangerous searches, which often result in addictions and self-destructive patterns.

What is obvious, yet not readily identified in our pursuit

or our apparent lack of pursuit, is that our humanity is fractured and broken. We are thirsty to complete ourselves. Our thirst seems insatiable. There is something within us individually and collectively that is inherently broken and seems irreparable. Though we try to fix it, try to complete ourselves, we fall short over and over again. We find we do not have the internal resources to mend ourselves, though we attempt and struggle to do it again and again.

Realizing our true identity, our God-given passions, and our purpose is the foundation of being complete, being fathered and finding home again. The extent to which they are unclaimed and unfulfilled or the extent to which they betray us is the extent that our incompleteness serves as a reminder of our homelessness and fatherlessness. The journey to identity, passion and purpose starts with recognizing that we are broken and in need of finding home again. It starts with a response to the invitation to community that has been highlighted throughout this book. The journey to community is a journey back to being connected, being fathered and finding home.

We are born separated from the source of life. We are born separated from the One Who loves us most and loves us best. We are born separated from living life the way it was meant to be lived. We are born disconnected and we awkwardly search for that place of connection our entire lives. We are born separated from the first community. Our journey to home begins with reconnecting to the source of life. That first community is a Trinity of persons: Father, Son and Holy Spirit.

We all live in a fatherless world. Physical orphans survive without a living father and emotional orphans survive with only a physical father. Because we are born spiritually fatherless, we are born spiritual orphans, cut off from our true identity, passions and our sense of purpose.

I was in Cebu City, Philippines, when I first identified

the universal cry of homelessness and fatherlessness. I had gone there to bring encouragement to a courageous team who had started a mid-wifery clinic among the poorest of the poor. The clinic (and eventual church) was launched by a team who, through relational contact, delivered the babies of those who would not receive medical attention otherwise. They also launched a feeding program each day where they would carefully weigh the food of the thirty or so malnourished children they were hoping to restore to health. The day often required a walk through the graveyard where the poor lived in squatter homes they had built.

While living among them for those few short visits, I was taken aback by seeing people living among the dead, their shacks around the tombstones and children playing on them as though they were part of a playground in the local park. As I looked into their eyes I could see their fatherlessness. I could see they did not know who they were, their fledging passions misdirected and their purpose reduced to survival.

On one hand it did not look much different than all of the spiritual fatherlessness I had seen in my life; it was just more pronounced. I heard it in their screams for affection as they displayed their talents, running through the graveyards awaiting my response and recognition. They wanted to be noticed, to be validated. As I later played a game of basketball with some teenage boys, whose nicknames were people we all know--Michael Jordan, Kobe Bryant and Vince Carter--I realized our worlds had a lot in common. As we played basketball together, I found myself acutely aware of their unclaimed identity and of their need to be fathered into purpose.

As I reflected in silence while absorbing my surroundings, I realized that we are all fatherless and homeless. It was the rawness of their reality that protruded into my space, helping me identify what was universal and common. They did not have the sophisticated methods to hide it or to cover it up as you or I might. They did not have access to comfort or the capacity to pacify their unclaimed identity, unfulfilled passion or betrayed purpose. They were looking for a home, for a father, just like all of us.

In Hong Kong I heard the same cry in the young men, or "brothers" as they are called at St. Stephens. Pioneered and led by Jackie Pullinger-To, St. Stephens has been a place where, for over thirty years, thousands of heroin addicts have seen their addictions severed by being reconnected to the One Who loves them most and loves them best --Jesus. It is a place where the maze of fatherlessness is traded in for a journey to claiming identity, fulfilling passions and discovering purpose. Each time I am there I am swallowed up in the intensity of their worship of God. In the desperation in their voices and the raw reality of their fatherlessness, I see a people who have touched reality.

Yet I realize they are only an expression of a universal longing, hidden to most of us. It is as though the veil of reality is thinner among the poor or those unable to cover their brokenness with acceptability. They are the ones closer to the universal reality the rest of us hide more effectively. They are the blessed ones in some ways. They are the ones who discover their brokenness because it is on public display and because their brokenness is unmanageable. Their false securities or false comforts are stripped away and they are able to find what many of us could not--the end of themselves and the reality of their need for connection to home and to the Father of all.

BROKENNESS

Our brokenness that results from our fatherlessness is most often expressed through our fears. We find out where we are broken by discovering what we fear most. When we fear we tend to control in order to contain our fear. Control is the closet door for our unwanted fears, locking them shut to others and to ourselves. Letting go of control by identifying our fears is one of the most significant processes in our journey to claiming our identity, fulfilling our passions and discovering our purpose.

Most of us do not live with the stories of heroin addicts in our daily lives or wild children in the graveyards of the Philippines, but we do live with our own brokenness wrapped up in our limited attempts to control it. We will do almost anything we can to stay in control, to keep our fear covered or protected.

However, taking control is an illusion. There is a difference between being in control and taking control. To be in control is being centered, or being self-controlled, but taking control is a response out of fear. We really cannot take control of our brokenness. We can only contain it. We can only hide it. Because our brokenness is not welcomed, we become unnatural as a society and hide from one another and from God.

Have you noticed that, for the most part, we in our Western culture tend to deny the realities that we do not control? We hide our sick and tuck them out of sight. We hide our elderly to keep from visiting our future. We hide our poor and homeless from fear that we might see ourselves in a mirror and become them. We hide our mentally handicapped to avoid our awkwardness and discomfort. We hide them because we hide it in ourselves. Unlike most cultures, we send our dead to "undertakers" to handle their disposal, to help us avoid facing this ultimate reality.

On the other hand, being in control is a process of letting go, of regaining the self-control we have lost. I was standing in the parking lot of a restaurant talking with a friend when, I was approached by a homeless man looking for breakfast. My friend tossed me a few coins and I took the man into the restaurant for a meal. We did not choose to stay as he did not want to be entertainment for the other customers, so we located another place to get a meal just a block away where he could sit in private. I sat across from him as he devoured his meal in my presence, somewhat seeing me as a necessary evil to achieve his end goal--food. I stayed because I wanted him to know I was not ashamed to be with him or to sit with him. I wanted to let him know I would embrace him.

Gary, as he called himself, proceeded to tell me how he was famous and everyone knew him or at least stared at him in this part of the city. He thought he should be charging a fee like everyone else does for services rendered. He proceeded to tell me about life on the street, his life on the street. He told me about the way of the poor. As I listened to this man, quite brilliant, quite articulate, yet obviously stuck in his pain, I was confronted with my own brokenness again.

Later I drove Gary to his destination. For ten minutes in an uninterrupted stream of consciousness he spoke about life, values and what really matters. I was confronted by his insight. He looked at me before departing and said, "Do you know why I ask people for money?"

I responded, "Not really."

He said, "Because it makes them go away."

I inquired further "Help me, Gary; I don't know what you mean by that."

He sat back and calmly said "Have you ever been in the forest with unwanted ants and bugs crawling on you and bees flying around you, requiring you to make a shelter around yourself to protect you from being harmed?"

I said, "Yes, I know what you mean."

He replied, "That is why I ask for money; it is my shelter to keep the bugs away. If I sit there they want to come into my space, but if I reach to them they will go away." He then looked at me, knowing I was a Christian, and said, "Will you pray for me before I leave?"

Having been quite touched by our encounter, I prayed for him before he departed.

In order to avoid "being in control," and maintain the habit of "taking control," our lives either shrink or expand. We either have to shorten the list of people we keep close to us or we have to get control over a vast number of people. Rather than living freely, experiencing life the way it was meant to be lived, we fight our brokenness, we fight our fear.

Though we do not often gain control by encountering people in ways as dramatic as described by Gary, who controls people by pushing them away, we do create shelters in more subtle ways. Our relational circles, our adventurous hearts, our love of exploration, our willingness to experiment become masked and placed behind the wall of control in case our fears escape us. When we live that way, our ability to claim our identity, fulfill our passions and discover our purpose slips from between our fingers and we remain fatherless and homeless in big ways and small ways. At minimum, we settle for survival and at best, maintain the status quo.

As we begin to trust God, the One who has control, we begin to gain what we initially lost—our self-control, and our journey continues. We are never completely free people until we find home on the inside and, until we start the journey back to community, by trading in our fatherlessness and homelessness for the journey to claiming our identity, unfulfilled passions and discovering our purpose.

WALKING IN BROKENNESS

"He who falls on this stone will be broken to pieces, but he on whom it falls will be crushed."[96] Jesus had been speaking at the time in parables, mysteries, to religious

people about His identity and His Father's intentions leading up to His arrival on earth. Jesus had been leading them to water as the saying goes, but they were not willing to drink. He impressed upon them the reality that unless they understood who He was—the rock on which their life was meant to be built—they would not recognize the foundation for identity. Their identity would be forever skewed and unclaimed.

Jesus invited them to community with Him. If they opened themselves to their brokenness and accepted it, they could fall on Him and be broken. It would wound and break them, but the alternative would be of greater severity. If they chose to hide in their insecurity, rather than facing their brokenness and being trained to walk in it with Christ, they would remain homeless and fatherless. If they hid in their brokenness, they would leave themselves vulnerable to the rock of life crushing them in dramatic or subtle ways. Jesus was indicating that the way of independence would ultimately lead them to becoming cynical, self-absorbed or over- protective.

The way of human beings is the way of dependence on the first community and then the community of others to claim our identity, passions and purpose. Yet life would have us believe the way of self-sufficiency is the road to living life the way it was meant to be lived, but it in actuality, it is the road to cynicism, narcissism or control.

While watching my twelve-year-old daughter Megan's recent sixth grade graduation ceremonies, I found myself questioning the process for how they were being rewarded. Were they rewarding the seeds of performance and self-sufficiency in the lives of these young people or as they meant to be doing—the seeds of confidence? I understand the goal and the intention of well-meaning people and a well-meaning process to reward positive behavior and talent. Yet I found myself wondering if the rewards achieve that outcome. Did it reward the talents and confidence that are emerging or did it reward performance and promote over-achievement? Did it help build confidence and overcome insecurities or did it move them further from relationship and community, which are the deepest longings of the heart?

I find myself watching an adult culture consumed with performance issues, trying to keep up, trying to win approval, and ask myself, who seeded this garden? Do ceremonies such as these contribute to the issues of performance in our formative years though the reward is tangible and confidence is built? Should we reward performance and perfection or should we reward vulnerability and dependence on community? Does it lead these young people to see their own brokenness and need of something greater than themselves or does it further support their growing capacity to sustain themselves from falling on the rock, ultimately leading them to an unmanageable reality? When these children discover they cannot hold it all together, will they then be crushed by the "rock" of life and become cynical, self-absorbed or over-protective to sustain their false reality?

Are we forced to become cynical about life, to become full of ourselves or over protect ourselves from awful things in order to survive? Was the permission to be real ever given? Will it keep them from walking in brokenness and opening their heart to life, or will it close in their world and tighten their grip to survive? If recognizing our brokenness is not cultivated, is it our narcissism that grows instead?

I am sure a ceremony of reward does many good things, but is the best lost in pursuit of the good? I am not sure I would be willing to take the role of judge and give a verdict of guilty or suggest we do away with such events, but I am left wondering and I am left pondering.

I grew up with a bent toward performance, with a

leaning toward self-sufficiency as a result of my childhood insecurities and brokenness. I was fertile ground for the seeds of independence because my spiritual homelessness and fatherlessness were acute. Growing up, I was quickly rewarded for my performance, for my achievements, for my success. I was rewarded for my strengths and for my leadership. The reward was approval, further success and opportunity. There was little place for anything less than self-sufficiency and my experiences further substantiated my worldview. Self-sufficiency and narcissism had gotten me this far in life, why would I want to cultivate anything less? I swallowed the hook early and became an over-achiever. I became driven to win approval, to achieve and to succeed. The side benefit was that I achieved in my school life, I was popular, successful and held in high regard. A year before my father's death and while in great personal upheaval I was voted *"Mr. Personality"* by all three ninth grade classes. In sports I was captain or co-captain often and in academics I strived hard.

Though I had become enviable in some people's eyes as a focused, resolute, and achieving young man, I was oblivious to the collateral damage along the way. My soul was paying a price I did not realize. While I was successful on one level, the level of achievement, the weight of responsibility in my young age robbed me from experiencing my complete identity. While on one hand aspects of my identity were being realized, other aspects, the deep relational part of me, were left hungry. I had vision but did not know how to be transparent. I knew how to be strong but did not know how to be weak. I was only self-aware in regards to my talents, gifts and vision. I was emotionally unaware of myself. I had no idea how I felt most of the time, as I was so preoccupied with achieving.

The social applause behind my pursuit spurred me on but left me wanting. I was given approval; I was given success and then defined by those. My brokenness and lack of self-awareness was disregarded and subtly applauded. What I really longed for in my soul was community, the place to be real, authentic and true but I didn't know how to get there. If I were ever weak would I be rejected and disregarded? I wondered. What I unconsciously feared was that my identity as a young man had become defined by my strength, by having it all together, not by being real along the way.

Many years of over-achievement gave me applause and success but kept me from aspects of my identity. I had a warm personality but connecting with any depth was difficult because I was blind to aspects of myself. We are emotional beings and we need to connect on more than the level of thoughts and ideas. We need to connect on the levels of emotion and who we are—transparency. I was largely unaware of my weaknesses and feelings; I was absorbed with me and unable to connect with others in a meaningful way. I was infected with the disease of performance and striving causing me to become self-righteous. I had to be strong but I found no freedom to be weak, to be broken. When I finally opened up and became honest about my emotions and deepest fears, I found it difficult to navigate through it as it required others and I had no resources as a young man for reaching out to others.

Once I faced another layer of my homelessness and fatherlessness I discovered uncharted territory in my unclaimed identity, my unfulfilled passions and my undiscovered purpose. Once I looked at my brokenness, I could begin to walk in brokenness and experience community. I chose to fall on the rock and continue to do so over and over again.

Robert and his common-law wife, Rebecca, had met a young man in our church community through their working relationship in the field of graphic arts. Through relationship, Robert and Rebecca eventually opened up their lives to spiritual things. During that time they personally encountered Jesus and the reality of their heroin addiction could not remain hidden. Rebecca had brought three children from a previous relationship into their relationship. The children were raised by the two of them during the time they were together.

At one point in our journey with them as a community we encouraged them to get married and they proceeded in that direction. During the week leading up to the wedding Rebecca moved out and stayed with Gary and Joy Best, pastors in our community, who first carried the relationship with them. Three days before the wedding Robert relapsed on heroin and overdosed in the Best's home. He was hospitalized for the night. I remember visiting him the next morning and seeing his condition. We encouraged them to hold off on the wedding, but they proceeded anyway. After that time they disappeared from community due to the hurt from our encouraging them to wait on the wedding.

Many months later they reappeared, searching for reconnection to God and community again. The community responded and initiated praying for them in their home. About three months later, after they were drug-free, I received an alarming phone call at 6:30 in the morning informing me that Rebecca was dead and Robert was devastated. I quickly called my friend in this process, Jeremy Wiebe, and the two of us went immediately to their home. We arrived to find the coroner in the bedroom placing Rebecca in a body bag, and Robert in the living room weeping with his parents by his side. The previous night they had decided to take a bit of heroin together, having been off it for several months. After they each used, Robert went into the living room and Rebecca into the bedroom. They had a pact where one would keep watch over the other when they used. At one point in the middle of the night she ended up over the toilet bowl throwing up, only to fall asleep there. Robert had decided to check on her and found her in the bathroom. He picked her up and put her in bed. Later that night he went again to check on her and discovered she had drowned in her vomit. Scared and shocked he called his parents and then us. There we all stood in the living room together in disbelief—Rebecca was dead. That week the birth father of the children took custody of his three children once he learned of Rebecca's death. Within one week Robert lost his wife and his three children. I remember doing the funeral of this twenty-seven year old mother of three who had died of a heroin overdose. I wondered if I could find any happy thoughts in this story. I wondered what I could say that would make a difference. I distinctly remember the audience, an underground drug world caught up in the same lifestyle. It was a very sad moment and yet a moment that would be etched in my mind forever.

One would think that would be enough to break Robert of his lifestyle and addictions, but it was not. He ran from community for five more months, smoking marijuana daily and binging on heroin, in part because he blamed himself for her death. One night about five months after her death, with his own peril in mind he carried out another act of self-destruction. After scoring more drugs, Robert drove to the nearby ocean's edge, a place where cliffs overlooked the ocean. He shot up again and decided to free-fall from the cliffs, hoping to end his life.

The next morning he awakened early in a pool of blood at the cliff's bottom as the tide was rolling in around him. He had finally fallen on the rock, this time it was literal, and it had broken him. In that moment, clarity of heart came to Robert. With several ribs broken he crawled back to his car deciding he must be alive for a reason. It was this time, when he had been broken to the core, that he found his way back to us and the journey to his freedom through community.

The journey to being broken had been secured now but the journey to walking in brokenness had only started. Soon after this time Robert and I were unaware of the next defining moment about to emerge from our conversation as we sat across the table from each other casually eating dinner together. I had taken Robert that day to a drug rehab center nearby to be freed from his heroin addiction. While we were there he appeared to be awkward, uncomfortable and even terrified at times.

"These people are not like me," he blurted out moments after being there. "They are far worse off than I and they have lived on the streets," he said to me as we were driving away following our short visit, "I just need a home and family to take me in. I don't need a place like that to get better."

I looked at him gently and said, "Do you want my help? If you do, you have to let go and trust the process to me."

He responded with more manipulative talk over the next couple hours as we drove around together. My hope was to simply endure the waves for the time being and not respond to him.

I knew as I looked across the restaurant table at him that I must demand his trust for this to work. While were eating together I said to him, "Do you want my help, Robert?"

He replied, "Yes."

I said. "Then we do it my way or you are on your own."

With tears welling up he knew I was immovable and he said what he was feeling and what I already knew: "I am so afraid. I have spent my whole life avoiding my pain and taking the easy road. I am scared to face it."

I said, "Why don't you ask Jesus what He wants you to do as He will be the one there with you in it."

That night Robert came home with me and stayed the

night. Before falling asleep, he randomly opened his Bible, asking God to show him what he should do with his life. The pages fell open to a story from the gospel of Matthew that illustrated how the man who built his house on the sand had it washed away in the storms but the man who built his house on the rock found it stood the test when the storms came.

As he read this passage he felt God told him he wanted to take his house, his life, that he had built completely on the sand, and put it on the Rock Christ Jesus. He then read the thoughts of Jesus prior to that story concerning the narrow road and the wide road. Robert realized in that moment that he had always tried to take the easy way. He felt God was inviting him to take the narrow road and face his pain.

When he told me this the next morning, I knew it would be a defining moment for his life if he would say yes to it. Robert would fall on the "rock" Jesus and be broken or the "rock" of life would again fall on him and he would be crushed as the scriptures teach. That morning we went to the rehab center.

Robert stayed in rehab for eight months, during which he came weekly to a home group in our house. His life was completely rebuilt, but it first had to be dismantled. It was a painful process that involved much grieving, many tears and time to heal. There were many trips he and I made back and forth together from my home to the center, talking together as we drove. There were many ups and downs, some difficult moments and some freeing moments. Community and role of community--both the rehab center and the church home group--were a significant part of his process to healing.

After much grieving and letting go, we wanted to see Robert take the next steps of growth for his life. He concluded he wanted to join YWAM (Youth With a Mission) to do a six-month discipleship school. Again we saw growth. He faced many more issues and fears, but pushed through them during his time with YWAM.

I remember the call I received from him after he had been in parts of Latin America for an outreach with his school. He had met street children who were sniffing glue and discovered he could empathize. For the first time in his life he felt alive and able to contribute to the greater good. After that experience he came home and worked two jobs for almost a year, paying restitution for his drug years and the losses he had caused. With his debts paid and a new freedom, he went off to Hong Kong to join St. Stephen's work for a year, supporting other heroin addicts' process to freedom.

At the writing of this book Robert is still working on rebuilding his life, but it is in a stable place. He will always walk with the limp of his own brokenness, as does anyone who has truly encountered the life-changing power of Christ. He has been drug free for over four years now, but most importantly he has hope and a future. Robert is on a journey through his brokenness to find his unclaimed identity, his unfulfilled passion and undiscovered purpose, and community has made the difference. Unfortunately for many like Robert, it takes a severe breaking to come to the end of themselves.

Whether our brokenness is protruding like Robert's for all to see, or hidden and even applauded like mine, learning to walk in our brokenness is a result of community. In some ways the strong and the successful are at a disadvantage, as it takes more of the weight of life to open them up to the need for community. It is not until we come to the end of our fierce independence and means to hold it all together, that we can even begin to understand community and the role of community in our lives. We often do not recognize our insatiable thirst as spiritual longings that can only be quenched by finding home and being fathered.

We must come to the place of willingly falling on the rock, which the Scriptures speak of as Jesus, to experience our brokenness. If we do not, the rock of the pressures of life will crush us into that reality. Those pressures will leave us cynical, self absorbed or over-protected to carry out our survival. Not everyone is as privileged as Robert. Not everyone has life bearing down to this magnitude on them, crushing and screaming for their attention. Robert is one of the blessed ones as the props of his life and the false securities were removed and the rock crushed him. Not everyone has life crush him in such an aggressive manner, nor would he or she willingly choose to face the brokenness.

Few of us experience the freedom of being completely loved and embraced——while still being imperfect. Even fewer of us discover that when we face our brokenness we are free to be human and free to grow in community. We hide much of whom we are from one another and therefore never experience community.

As a pastor I often see the other side of people's lives. I get to see the bottom side of the carpet with all its loose ends exposed while most experience the other side of the carpet of people's lives. I have discovered that we end up living in our false realities with one another, never entering into our brokenness for fear of rejection. We seldom feel free to experience life apart from holding it all together on the outside.

When we are free to walk in our brokenness we are free to begin to experience community and we are free to begin the journey to our unclaimed identity, our unfulfilled passions and our undiscovered purpose. When we don't walk in our brokenness, we live the life we were never meant to live, homeless and fatherless. We live our life being broken, not learning to walk in our brokenness.

Chapter 7
Process Questions

1. How have your dealt with your "fatherlessness and homelessness" in unhealthy ways?

2a. If "taking control" is a response of fear in what areas of your life are you "taking control"?

2b. Once you have identified that ask yourself, what am I afraid of?

3. When/if the "rock" of life has crushed you how have you learned to walk in brokenness as a result?

4. In what ways has control (over protecting yourself) narcissism (self – love) or cynicism (being critical), affected your journey to identity, passion and purpose?

5. What could be your next step to walking in greater brokenness?

CHAPTER 8
COMMUNITY BEGINS IN YOU

THE FIRST COMMUNITY

In order to respond to the invitation to community we must understand who it is that defines community and who it is that invites us. God is community. He defines its fundamental nature and is the leading community. The community of Father, Son and Holy Spirit live together with no fear of the other and with the complete and full embrace of the other. Neither ambition nor competitiveness exists between them. They celebrate one another and applaud one another with no fear of consequence. One's approval does not magnify loss in another in the first community. They are complete in love. This community of three persons, Father, Son and Holy Spirit are complete in love and can freely love one another without fear.

Being broken means fear has penetrated us and its poison has infected us. Those traces of fear left inside us are in opposition to community. When we fear, it is because we are not made complete in love. *"If we are afraid, it is for fear of judgment, and this shows that His love has not been perfected in us."*[97] We cannot love another until we know we are loved. The depth of our experience of the love of this first community determines the depth of which community can be formed in us. When we receive His invitation to His community we are accepting an invitation into a living and experiential reality. It is not a legend, it is not a belief we hold fast to, it is a living reality practiced in our daily lives. We are being invited to come home, to come into the process of completion. We are invited to be a member of this existing and fear-free community. Our entry into this community changes us. Their completeness begins to transform us and works in us, making us ready to love and be loved.

It prepares us to enter the second community, other people, which has traces of fear in it. When we have connected with the first community we are protected from annihilation. Up until this connection is made we are restlessly alone in the world and intuitively aware that we must protect ourselves from destruction by another. Yet when we enter in the first community we realize we can never be destroyed. We can be hurt, mistreated, wounded and painfully rejected in community but we cannot be annihilated because we have found home, we have found the Father. Any community that does not find its source in the first community will ultimately not succeed and will eventually implode. Community void of the first community cannot sustain itself with the toxic level of our combined brokenness heaped together.

Our journey begins in us when we experience the first community. As a member of His community we can begin our journey to our unclaimed identity, our unfulfilled passions and our undiscovered purpose. As we set in motion that journey on the inside, then others can come around us and can occupy various roles to further complete our journey. It also allows us to occupy that role in another's life and allows us to play a part in the script of another's unfolding journey to identity, passion and purpose. We can more readily recognize it in those coming behind us, in our next generation, because we can see it in ourselves. It is the security of our place in the first community that gives way to the courage required to enter into the transparency, honesty and openness necessary to enter the second community. When we open ourselves to others, we open ourselves to be hurt, to be misunderstood and to be further pained.

Yet in opening ourselves to pain we open ourselves to love. When we open ourselves to love we are opening ourselves to being made complete in love. This is part of the journey required to experience our unclaimed identity, our unfulfilled passions and our undiscovered purpose. It is fear that keeps us from being made complete and from helping to further the completion of others. It is fear of being destroyed that keeps us from community. Yet the fatherlessness in us can find the Father and the homelessness a home in the first community. The Father longs to tell us who we are, where we belong while He gives us a context to discover his purposes for our lives. While others participate on the stage of our life it is God who writes our script.

THE LIMITATIONS OF ONE

C.S. Lewis' *Voyage of the Dawntreader*, one of the books in the Narnia series, Lewis imagines a ship's journey encountering a variety of islands along the way. Each island's people and culture were filled with unique stories. Each island's people and culture were masterfully crafted to depict the distinct characteristics of what it means to be human. Lewis' fiction touches our reality in a most subtle and profound way.

And, in a way, Lewis' fantasy was transformed into reality for our group. Sixty-five of us--adults, teenagers and families--began stringing up our hammocks for the long anticipated twelve day journey up the Amazon River through Brazil's remote jungles. Most of us were Canadian, including our three-month-old baby girl, Megan, and not at all prepared for what we would encounter. *General Osorio III* was the name of our ship. She did not have the eloquence of the *Dawntreader* or her magic, but rather the loud roar of her four-cylinder engine and a handful of dedicated

Brazilian crewmembers to take her to destiny.

Our voyage began with the anticipation of the unknown pushing us down the river. We looked forward to the discovery of a variety of port cities, unaware that each would have its own distinct culture and message, all Brazil, yet all so unique.

In Itaguitcihara we found ourselves secluded in a world caught in time. We peered down the streets in the scorching heat only to find horse carts and horses going about their routine of transporting people, pigs living the lives of the American family dog and McDonalds only being identified as a farm.

We had gone with the hope of bringing practical service by building homes and handing out food to those in need. In addition, we shared an invitation, through art and dance, to unearth their thirst for something real. The public schools, en masse, awaited our arrival as the first outside visiting group to their world. What a privilege it was to be in this unique part of Brazil.

Five hundred miles from the ocean's edge lay the port of Santarem, the Amazon's finest. Unlike other parts of Brazil, Santarem did not show the pollution of the region and the poverty of the Amazon Basin. Cleanliness is its aroma and the future is its now. The church in Santarem was alive and growing and the people inquisitive. The people's curiosity allowed us to gather large crowds wherever we went.

Though a little city, Parintins had a bold and sensual personality. Lured by the mystic of the city's atmosphere, each year multitudes of people would come to celebrate her renowned festival. Established in 1793, this river city of one hundred thousand people is known the world over for the largest cultural expression in Brazil held each June. Lost in the tributaries of the Amazon, Parintins would host the thousands of people, who had come to be fattened by festivity.

Boats from everywhere came to fill the place as thousands of people poured into this city for the *Festival of the Bulls*. During the month of June the city is divided into two. One half of the city carries allegiance to the red bull and the other half to the blue bull. In this month-long festival, momentum is gained for a final and deciding competition over who will carry the city's superiority, the red bull or blue. The bull is a large costumed head connected by a trellis of people depicting the bull's body and tail. It is a choreographed dance, a synchronized motion and a generation's long folklore all wrapped together. During the month of June the spirit of that city erases neutrality from its vocabulary. Everyone must choose a bull. As the folklore engages into full gear the one time friend becomes enemy and beatings and stoning occur when geographic boundary lines are crossed.

In July, Parintins returns to normal. Life was ordinary upon our arrival in July of that year. It was the aftermath of a party that greeted us. Hollowness filled the air as the echoes from the festivities still rang through the streets. Fattened with her fill of festivity, Parentins fell asleep awaiting the return of her Prince to awaken her again next year.

My view as an outsider caused me to be perplexed by the apparent lack of regard for another and the lack of reflection over the impact of this festival. Brother hating brother, beatings, bribery, and betrayal filled the hearts of people trying to fulfill an uncontested folklore. Festival judges were escorted out of harm's way before the final results were announced in fear of the repercussions. A festival? I asked myself. What would make a peaceful people live in such a way without questioning the validity of their activities?

Without reflection in our lives we are vulnerable to misdirection because the voices around us can be large, loud and all consuming. Deep in the Amazon, this city called Parintins reveals the impact of the lack of reflection in our lives. The voice of this folklore in Brazil seems so loud and rooted that it goes unquestioned year after year. We may pass judgment as outsiders on such an event easily, while asking ourselves how they could not see the effects of this folklore on their lives and relationships. However the flaws we may readily identify in another's culture we overlook in our own if we are not given to reflection.

One uncharted area of reflection in the culture of the west is our indiscriminate acceptance of rugged individualism as the way life was meant to be lived. The *power of one* as it is often heralded is the center of our folklore. It may not come in a festival of costumed bulls but rather from numerous sources and dressed in countless attire. Yet it is no less an unrestrained full embrace of an unchallenged appeal to our fatherlessness and our homelessness, disguised as the way of the successful. The power of one is the spoken words echoing throughout our culture's canyons. Rugged individualism is rewarded, applauded and made legendary in the annuals of our culture's history. These are our culture's heroes and heroines, not the red and blue bull. They are the loners, the self-made, those who rise above the crowd on their own power and of their own making. Having been the hero, the so-called self-made person, I find the foundation of this worldview faulty and left wanting.

Heroes are in actuality not self-made; that defies the real meaning of being a human hero. We cannot make ourselves, and if we suppose we have, it is to the detriment, and not the benefit of others. Relationships become the causalities of our devotion to the belief in the power of one. We may rise above the crowd but by ourselves and for ourselves.

The strong are meant for the weak not for themselves. Like the Amazonian city, Parintins, this worldview is robed in sensuality as she flaunts her beauty. Little yet bold, she lures the multitudes with her mystic. The power of one is an attractive voice in our culture. Her mystic is in opposition to our journey to our true identity, passion and purpose.

Community serves as an authentic voice that echoes silently in our culture. It echoes to the limitations of one. As human beings we were made with only two eyes on one side of our being. We were born with limitations to what we can see at any given moment. We are born with limitations to see ourselves accurately and fully. We can be seen by another more fully than we can see ourselves. We are born blind to our full reality and it is only in community that we can discover the dimensions of ourselves, our God-given passions and our purpose.

Some of those discoveries are painful as they expose our denial and our blindness. While others of those discoveries are liberating as they speak to our uncertainty and call us into greater certainty regarding our identity, passions and purpose. Without community we are left to our one-dimensional view of ourselves. We are left to grope in our darkness, sometimes never knowing and more importantly, never finding.

There are multiple ways in which community serves to support us on the journey to identity, passion and purpose. Drs. Henry Cloud and John Townsend, in their book, *How People Grow*, said, "One of the most valuable processes in life is grief. In life, we basically digest experience; we walk through it, take it in, use what is useful, and eliminate the waste.... Grief can only be accomplished in the context of [community]. We need others to hold us as we go through the process of letting down and letting go." It is community that serves the grieving process. Community also serves the purpose of connection and our need for accountability. Cloud and Townsend go on to say, "Accountability is not a cure for lack of self-control."[98] When we are in need of healing, accountability with others serves as point of reference for that assessment.

Community is also the place where we experience grace and forgiveness, which are requirements for our reaching identity, passion and purpose. It is in community that we are mentored, in which we experience the modeling of how to do life in ways that we lack training. Community shows us the limitations of one person and shocks us into the reality of our necessity for others.

Isolation is a disease. It is the disease of a culture that has swallowed the belief that success is reached by achieving rugged individualism. We may actually reach success through being rugged individualists but the price tag is high. It leaves us shallow and feeling hollow because we are left lonely and dying on the inside. We find success but lose meaning because that is not the way life is meant to be lived.

THE ROOSTER'S CROW -
THE WAY OF COMMUNITY

It is a tale of two communities. One could hear rumbling in the air as the multitudes of working men awakened to the crowing of the rooster. The clanging of chains in mass unison, the roar of thousands of chariot wheels in motion, the wisp from the swirling dust clouds hurtling by as thousands of men marched to the quarry followed each mornings awakening. In this Egyptian land, the Hebrew slaves would awaken day after day at a precise time, to a preset routine and to a predestined outcome. For nearly four hundred years the Hebrew slaves' unwelcome lifestyle secured their provision and shelter, but cost them their freedom.

Recently this extraordinary and remarkable story of

freedom was revisited and brought to the forefront of our culture in DreamWorks epic movie *The Prince of Egypt*. It portrayed the monumental account of the exodus of the Hebrew people out of slavery described in the book of Exodus. We were spellbound by its miracles, intrigued by its unassuming beginnings and caught up in the innocence of its characters' lack of awareness of the story's ending.

Where this story ends in the movie *Prince of Egypt* is where I want to begin. A people set free, a people now broken of routine and ready to taste what they had only dreamed of. With their expectations high and their hopes large they embarked into the wilderness with Moses as their leader. They had never been there before. They had certainly not lived without routine, without provision, and without the security of someone directing their lives in a predetermined manner.

They had a vision of freedom in their mind's eye and yet a different reality would soon emerge. Freedom was not their exercising the right of control as they had so anticipated but rather the freedom to discover community. Once outside the walls of routine and direction, their freedom destroyed them, as they had never functioned freely with one another or with themselves.

Their previous lifestyle was controlled from the outside. They merely had to know the rules and keep the rules. The rules were now gone and all they had was an uncharted journey to community. They had a vision of personal freedom that did not include the reality of taking personal responsibility. They did not know how to take responsibility for their lives. Up until this time their experience of community had been limited. It had been precipitated by connecting around a common enemy, the Egyptian people and their Pharaoh. Now they had no enemy and no initial rationale, other than the hope of being free.

In their pursuit of freedom they become conscious of

their togetherness and of their God. Their wilderness experience soon became more about the process to community rather than the process to freedom. But sadly, after forty years of wandering in the wilderness, as the story is told, they by no means had entered into community and certainly did not attain the promise. They wanted to kill their leader Moses at times, and they complained about their provision or lack of it at other times. They went in circles, never being free from their past. The oppression of Egypt within them did not remain in Egypt but rather stayed with them. They never made it through the phases of developing community, but stayed stuck in the process of ever-searching yet never grasping freedom and her intention.

If we fast-forward through time, we see a similar story with a different outcome. Scripture is God's story of our story. And in the New Testament, we come across a motley crew of people called together with the hope of freedom, but again experiencing the unanticipated process of community.

Each one of these men had been personally selected by the one who would lead them.[99] Each one had concerned himself with Who had called them out in his life and not with whom he was called alongside. It was of colossal proportions for each of them to discover who had also been selected along with them. Only Christ had understood the invitation to the twelve disciples that he had called into the way of community.

Preoccupied with being selected, they were emotionally unprepared to enter into community with others. It was Christ they were responding to and apprenticing under, not eleven other people. Yet it was the new community that Christ was forming, not just their individual connection that preoccupied His vision for them. He was concerned with their togetherness as much as they were concerned with their individual relationship with Him.

We see in their unfolding journey how community

played a role in their discovery of identity, passion and purpose. As they first gathered, one can almost predict their awkwardness. Their silence speaks of their scrutiny of one another.

In the early stages of community it is our silence, our politeness, and our hope for a good experience that keeps us from honesty and from beginning to form community. M. Scott Peck in his book *A Different Drum* writes, "The essential dynamic of pseudocommunity is [our] conflict avoidance"[100]. Our differences are not yet out in the open, they lay in silence. How could the twelve followers of Christ not have had differences, based on their places in society?

There was a handful of ruling families in which the Herods ruled Galilee and Trans-Jordan at that time. Under the reign of Herod the Jewish people were allowed to govern themselves for the most part except in two areas where the reality of their oppression was experienced. They lived with the reality of a foreign army present in the affairs of their lives and an oppressive tax system was set up to ensure that the strong remained strong.

What made the tax system oppressive is that it offered a premium for extortion and plundering. The Roman censor sold franchises to the highest bidder for taxes. He would set a quota for the government and left the tax collector freedom to collect open-ended commission. A tax collector was a Jew who was used as a tool of the oppressive hand of Rome and the tax collectors were cheating their own people with the backing of Rome. Tax collectors were excluded from Jewish society simply because of their occupation.

Levi, one of those Jesus invited to be with him, was a tax collector. It appears Levi was primarily a collector of custom and duties on goods entering the Herodian territory crossing the Jordan when Jesus Christ called him. Levi more than likely collected taxes from the other disciples at some point. I am sure the others were puzzled, if not offended, to see Him sitting beside them.

Many communities stay their entire existence in this stage of community because they do not allow their differences out in the open with one another. In any family or any community that has "no talk" rules or topics that are inferred as off bounds for discussion, community is limited. Our ability to experience community is limited in proportion to our accessibility and in proportion to the number of "no talk" rules.

Once our differences are invited out into the open, community begins to take shape in us. Our openness and honesty sit as opposites on the scale of our individuality and independence. The scales will tip one way or the other in this developing stage of community. Either we move forward into community or remain in pseudocommunity. Stepping into self-disclosure and honesty require safety to speak out our differences. The subconscious question being asked by the disciples and anyone entering community is, 'How far will I go with these people'?

M. Scott Peck says, "The basic pretence of pseudo-community is the denial of individual differences.... Once you've found God, then you don't need to be afraid anymore"[101], one member says to the group. A remark like this, though potentially true when spoken as a personal statement, weakens community when spoken as a general statement because it ignores the language of community and pushes our differences aside. Peck goes on to say, "Individuals think to themselves, I found God twenty years ago and I'm still scared, but why let the group know that?"[102] The language of community is a personal language. A comment spoken in those terms implies that I have not found God if I am still afraid. This further isolates us from one another and compromises group safety.

When a comment of this nature is ignored by the larger

community at the risk of conflict or hurting someone's feelings, the community remains immature and further community is compromised. Though the Scriptures do not give us exact dialogue referencing the disciples going through this stage, one can just imagine the thoughts, the unspoken head noise, and the internal conflict that existed among them.

It took time together with them for Jesus to create the safety needed for them to enter into eventual conflict and the chaos required for progress. Again, it was Scott Peck who said, "Chaos is not just a state; it is an essential part of the process of community development."[103] We get snapshots of some of their conflict among the disciples when it says, *"An argument started among the disciples."*[104] Not only were their differences out in the open but also their hearts were exposed as they were arguing about who was the greatest. At this stage of growing into community our differences are out in the open, but we have not taken responsibility for our feelings or thoughts yet. We want to hold others responsible, but not ourselves.

Sometimes the leaders are the scapegoat, sometimes the community is the scapegoat, and sometimes other enemies are identified as the point of reference for our denial in conflict. Once we realize the enemy is within us and is our barrier to communication, we can begin to move into the most vital stage of forming community, emptying ourselves. When we empty ourselves of our barriers we begin to see one another more clearly. Peck says, "Until such a time as we can empty ourselves of expectations and stop trying to fit others and our relationships with them into a preconceived mould we cannot really listen, hear, or experience."[105]

It is embracing our brokenness and our shame that allows us to take responsibility for our thoughts and feelings more readily. When we are uncertain that we are loved at that deepest part of us, it is hard for us to enter into community. Yet it can be community that heals our identity in this way and proves love to us.

In Matthew's gospel Peter had declared to his community that he would never deny Jesus even if the rest of his disciples did.[104] He let his differences out into the open with twelve witnesses, including Jesus standing by to authenticate it. Peter was confident in himself and his commitment to follow through. Yet Peter had not spoken in the full language of community because he had not yet emptied himself of himself.

At that moment, Jesus as leader of that forming community, tried to prepare Peter and others for Peter's eventual demise. Peter, almost indignant, responded by saying *"even if I have to die with you I will never disown you."*[107] By then the rest of the community was caught up in Peter's resolve and joined him in his declaration.

Later on that day the disciples witnessed Peter's humiliation and then their own as he disowned Jesus publicly. The crow of the rooster announced Peter's brokenness to both him and his community, just as Jesus predicted. The rooster's crow reminded Peter and reminded the others of their humanity. Peter and then the other disciples, one by one, slipped from community as the unpredictable and unnerving events of the crucifixion of Christ unfolded before their eyes.

Caught in their chaos, their self-declarations and their conflict, this budding community was fraying at the end, or was it? Maybe this is the natural process of forming community. Maybe one stage of community requires us to look at our brokenness in the presence of others to enter into the fullness of community and the fullness of our identity, passions and purpose.

This stage of community utilizes our broken humanity to heal us and to open us to one another, as our actions will reveal us when our hearts are not willing. Our strengths, as we have seen with Peter's strength of courage to declare his commitment, often set the stage for our humanity to pierce through and be known. Our strengths often make way for our brokenness to be exposed. It is our recognition of weakness, not strength, that makes us capable of being in community.

Our weaknesses, when exposed, leave us embarrassed and our humiliation bids us to hide. When we face our humanity we find a greater understanding of our unclaimed identity, our unfulfilled passions and our undiscovered purpose because it's within community they are best defined and experienced. When we see our own brokenness more clearly we have grace for another because grace has been extended to us. When we accept our brokenness we have emptied ourselves of ourselves and have room for another.

When Peter re-entered his community I am sure he re-entered with a greater awareness of his own humanity. I am sure he entered with a greater awareness of his limitations and his need for community. The accountability of community precipitated Peter's identity coming into focus, his passions being refined and his purpose about to be unleashed, but not this side of the emptying of himself.

The way of community is the way of walking into synergy—becoming more than the sum of our parts. Into the environment of transparency and humility, where this community that had faced their brokenness and emptied themselves, came one of the most historic stories of a people who became more than themselves. Written in the book of Acts we see the marks of this missional community. We see ordinary people becoming more than themselves.

We leave the book of Acts spellbound by its miracles, intrigued by its unassuming beginnings, and caught up in the innocence of its characters' lack of awareness of the story's ending. The community of Hebrew slaves did not reach their destiny while the second community of unlearned disciples did. The difference between the community of Christ's disciples and the community of the freed Hebrews slaves is that the former became a missional community, while the latter got stuck in the process of chaos. When we hear the rooster's crow in our life, we need to recognize the invitation to embrace our brokenness. When we begin to embrace our brokenness we can begin to embrace the way of community.

BECOMING A MISSIONAL COMMUNITY

After this moment in his life Peter became focused, refined and unleashed, as did the other disciples. The difference was they had experienced the effects of community and the impact of community in finding their unclaimed identity, unfulfilled passions and undiscovered purpose. Peter, along with ten of the other eleven disciples, responded to the invitation to connect to the first community. In their connection to the first community they exchanged their fatherlessness and homelessness for the journey to their true identity, passion and purpose. In their experience with being with one another these eleven disciples became a trophy for how to become more than themselves together, a missional community. At times they fought against each other and the process, and at others times it was exciting and adventurous. It was confusing and chaotic in certain instances, yet community was bringing them all to the edge of their identity, passions and purpose.

As the book of Acts unfolds we are invited to taste of the culmination of their lives together. Individually and collectively they discovered who they were, where they belonged and what their purpose on earth was all about. It was not what they did, although it was noteworthy and marked history, but rather it was what they became—focused, refined and unleashed—which mattered most.

I love Gene Edwards' description of what happened to Peter. "Simon Peter was a commercial fisherman. He was about thirty years old when he met Jesus. For most of his life he had the reputation of a filthy-tongued, joking, shallow, loud-mouthed braggart." While listening to John the Baptist, Peter fell under great distress. "John's words hit him like a hammer, Peter crumbled."[106] Peter was awakened to being full of himself and his disconnection with God. "A few months later Simon [Peter] had gone out to hear and to meet yet another prophet – Jesus the Nazarite. Sporadically he followed Jesus around. Finally, entranced by what he saw and heard, he began following the Lord everywhere, night and day. For the next three and half or four years, Simon Peter was never out of sight of the Lord. He lived and breathed, ate and slept in the constant presence of Jesus."[109] His life was changed forever.

His experience within community proved him nevertheless to still be rather dull and thick headed. He was predictably spontaneous, yet at times brash and disconnected. He was willing but weak, strong but penitent. His denial of Jesus within his community and within his own heart broke him, but the cross and the three days to follow changed all that. Peter was walking in brokenness at last, he had seen himself and emptied himself; he was ready for new dimensions of experiencing his identity, passion and purpose. Each of the other disciples, except Judas Iscariot, all had similar experiences to Peter's as they, too, became aware of their brokenness.

It was this man, a man aware of his brokenness and the eleven others, including Judas's replacement that stood up on the opening act of church history. *Then Peter stepped forward with the eleven other apostles and shouted to the crowd, "Listen carefully, all of you, fellow Jews and residents of Jerusalem. Make no mistake about this. Some of you are saying these people are drunk. It is not true. It's much too early in the morning. No, what you see this morning was predicted centuries ago by the prophet Joel: In the last days, God said, I will pour out my Spirit upon all people. Your sons and daughters will prophesy, your young men will see visions, and your old men dream dreams. In those days I will pour out my spirit upon all my servants, men and women alike...."*[110]

Gene Edwards, in *Revolution* tells us, "The number of foreigners present in the city [Jerusalem] is a mind – boggling five hundred thousand. They have jammed into every square inch of the one square mile that is Jerusalem." At that time Jerusalem was like a present day New York. People had travelled from all over the Roman Empire to join in the great celebration of this Jewish tradition, Pentecost. "Their native tongues are Greek, Latin or one of a dozen other languages spoken in the empire." That morning the disciples and over a hundred other people had gathered for a prayer meeting as Christ told them to do before he ascended to heaven nine days earlier. "All morning, since dawn, the pilgrims had been passing without interruption down this street, past the upper room where the disciples were gathered, and out into the temple grounds. The procession had come to an abrupt halt. They had heard a faint rumbling sound in the sky. Looking up, they listened and waited. Gradually the sound had grown into an ear-shattering roar-like sound of wind blowing at hurricane velocity. As they listened they began to realize that the sound was moving earthward. It seemed to be headed for the two-story house right on the edge of the temple grounds.... Every eye was glued to that second story room. In the next moment a door opened and a man shot out of the room. He began calling to people in the street, speaking in his native Galilean dialect."

Then, to everyone's amazement another Galilean shot out speaking in flawless Greek, then another in Latin and Egyptian, all speaking in regards to the Messiah, Christ. "The people on the street were dumbfounded. No one had ever heard anything like it. Somebody just had to yell out from the crowd 'They're all drunk'. The crowd laughed with relief." "History was being made by the minute. Only a few moments ago the very spirit of the Lord had come down and clothed man! Within the same hour the *Kingdom of God*, a Kingdom that until this time had confined itself to the realm of the heavens, had moved to earth. But the greatest event of all this was: The church had been born!" [111] The church is less than one hour old and Peter is the first to step upon the stage of her history.

The church was born in weakness, not strength, as Peter and then others were born in weakness, not strength. This community called the Church was born out of their collective experience with real community. Their identity was made known through connecting to the first community, walking in brokenness, realizing their individual limitations and then discovering the way of community.

In this defining and unanticipated moment Peter and the others walked into the beginnings of experiencing missional community – community becoming fully alive. The mission of a community is to bring others into community with God; inviting them to trade their homelessness and fatherlessness for a journey to identity, passion and purpose. They were now inviting others into the community they had experienced. They were no longer focused on themselves but on others and were prepared to serve others with the embrace of their own identity, passion and purpose.

Most of us will not experience this breadth of influence or historical presence in our journey to discovering our identity, passion and purpose. That, however, does not make our discovery illegitimate or of a lesser value. Although we are giving the account of a world changing missional community and people who have found their place marked in history, it is not their greatness that calls to us. It is the simplicity of their discovery that invites us. Their story invites us to consider that this same discovery is within our reach. It was the growing awareness of their disconnection from the Father coupled with the realization of their individual limitations that made their discovery reachable. Their response to this growing awareness involved an increased commitment to embracing their brokenness and the courage to be transparent and vulnerable within community. It is this simplicity that dares us and calls us to discovery.

It is the mission of community that allows us to reach our potential. This same Peter later brought the mission of community to a sharpened point in his own writings recorded in the Scriptures *"But you are not like that, for you are a chosen people. You are a kingdom of priests, God's holy nation, His very own possession. This is so you can show others the goodness of God, for he called you out of the darkness into his wonderful light."*[112]

God invites us all to be his priests, his kingdom of priests, "priests without robes, without temples, without training, without hierarchical status. A priest presents a person to God, or represents God to a person. A priest makes the God connection verbal or visible."[113] "There are a variety of offices in the community of faith--prophet, priest, wise person, elder, apostle, deacon, bishop--but throughout the church, the primary emphasis is on the people."[114]

We are called to be a *"kingdom of priests,"* a people whose mission is to serve as priests, the Old Testament scriptures declare and the New Testament writings confirm. Community is meant to be a place where we become priests, not just a place to have priests. We are called to this kind of community living. Community serves the process of mission in this way. It serves as the role for spiritual growth. When the whole community participates in one another's spiritual growth, missional community evolves. Jean Vanier describes it this way. "The mission of a community is to give life to others, that is to say, to transmit new hope and new meaning to them. Mission is revealing to others their fundamental beauty, value and importance in the universe, their capacity to love, to grow and to do beautiful things and to meet God."[115]

My wife, Maryanne, works as a registered nurse in the local hospital. She often is invited into revealing the fundamental beauty, value and importance of people to themselves. People in a hospital are vulnerable, often open and in need of reassurance. They are in a place to receive love–hers and God's. I recall one instance when she was caring for a terminally ill lady who had been receiving heavy doses of pain medication. The lady was still experiencing severe emotional pain while on medication. Maryanne would often go in her room and gently just lay her hand upon her shoulder, praying silently. The love transferred and the beauty expressed did not go unnoticed. While laying in pain on one occasion this lady, with tears streaming down her face looked up at Maryanne and asked, "Are you an Angel?" Maryanne just smiled at her.

"No, I am not. I am praying for you because God cares for you and loves you," she replied. Maryanne was making the God connection verbal and visible to her.

The journey to experience and pass on identity, passion and purpose begins in community and ends in community. It begins in the mission of God and ends in our personal response to His mission. Our journey out of homelessness and fatherlessness towards identity, passion and purpose calls us to participate in community, His community first.

BEGINNING THE JOURNEY
TO MISSIONAL COMMUNITY

For many who have experienced "church," they have not yet experienced community, at least the reality of a missional community defined in the journey we have just gone through together. Church and community, as we have defined them, are not interchangeable words in many of our vocabularies and experiences. Church has been something we attend, contribute to or serve, while real community and real mission is something that happens elsewhere in our lives, if it happens at all. If the fullness of our identity, passion and purpose are discovered within community how do we get there? How do we as individuals and we as a collective make that transition from what we are to what we want to be?

While the longing for missional community begins in our hearts it is only worked out in our relationships, our relationship with God and then others. Missional communities demand each participant to take initiative and to recognize the value of their contribution. It necessitates that each participant ask themselves what they are really committed to as they will walk in uncertainty and pain in relationship.

It also requires that both facilitators of community and participants in community *"stay at the table"* when brokenness emerges. The first disciples had to learn how to *"stay at the table"* when their feelings were hurt, when they felt rejected or abandoned by each other. Peter and then the others reconnected, after they abandoned one another and disowned Christ. They forgave one another and walked in their brokenness together. If we are committed to remain open and honest in conflict, to own our *stuff*, and to not use our position of influence or our clout in relationships to control communication, we can begin this journey with others.

In missional communities where people are discovering their identity, passion and purpose, the following elements will be present. Missional communities will foster a culture of mentoring relationships, a culture of personal initiative and a culture of interactive dialogue. Often we are looking for a mentor rather than mutually mentoring one another. An autocratic leader cannot foster a mentoring community and an unresponsive participant cannot experience being a mentor. When participants wait to be recruited, wait to be asked to take initiative in relationship, they thwart the process of mission in their lives and in community.

Often we are looking for someone to tell us what to do rather than taking initiative towards one another and often we are looking to be told how to do something rather than thinking, feeling and growing together. Breaking out of our passivity and our low self esteem is vital to this process. Unfortunately we have become a society of professionals, specialists and experts rather than a society of contributors and participants. We have been told we don't know.

Missional communities are trying to lift the level of participation in transparent community and in authentic personal mission. Missional communities are defined by life change, not by numbers. They are defined by movement and growth in individual lives not solely by the quality of their programs. Missional communities move slower in terms of the quantity of growth on the front end but deeper and more effective on the quality of growth during their life span. Missional communities allow for and require initiation by individuals in a community towards the people in their existing spheres of influence. Jesus said *"And here is how to measure it – the greatest love is shown when people lay down their lives for their friends."*[116] As my friend, David Ruis, often says "Jesus is not asking for sacrifice in our missional living as love takes us beyond sacrifice and duty, where even our enemies we now embrace in the spirit of friendship, laying our lives down for them." Jesus is simply calling us to honest and transparent relationship, and to embrace the spirit of friendship. He is saying there is no greater love than to lay down our lives in the spirit of friendship. The Kingdom and its mission begin and end in love and so should our lives.

If I am a stay at home mom I look for those around me in my present sphere (likely other mothers) that God is connecting to me, so I can recognize His working and join with Him in the spirit of friendship. If I am an employer, an employee or a student, I too, must ask God for "eyes to see" those around me and what He is doing in my life and enter through the spirit of friendship. I must then cultivate those relationships as they will not just happen. I ask God to show me in the spirit of friendship where individuals are in their own spiritual journey so I can share and participate with them. Friendship requires that I share myself with others not just my knowledge about God.

"The church became redefined as a community spawned by the mission of God and gathered up into that mission."[117] In mission we do not bring God anywhere or to anyone. When evidence of God already at work in peoples lives is not present, we should not presume their hearts are ready. We recognize as Jesus did *My Father never stops working..."* [118] Being missional and being a missional community is not simply the bringing of knowledge but rather the joining with, in the spirit of friendship, the activity of God in the world. Missional communities are all about recognizing the mission of God in the world and joining with Him.

Getting to the place of being a missional community involves the equipping of people, the releasing of catalysts and the experience of the collective. The role of leadership in missional communities is to empower people, to identify participants who can equip and release others through relationship and to offer a place for people to grow through the experience of their togetherness. When leaders relate to people from positions of authority and not relational authority, which is earned through love and service, they shut down the process of missional community. A group culture that does not invite our differences into the open or that has "no talk" rules will only remain a leader centered group or a program driven experience.

No matter where we are today in this journey the challenge is to acknowledge it in our lives and in our collective experience. It is not that we want to allow ourselves to be overwhelmed by where we are not in this journey but rather it is about our *coming to life*.

Once we identify where we are on this journey we will have already launched into being vulnerable. Though if only with ourselves, it is the first step in our *coming to life*. Outfitted with the experience of being vulnerable we are then ready to wade through the waters of the next step.

The next step involves the repair of our part in the collective experience. We cannot come to life on our own – it is together that we find our journey to identity, passion and purpose. If we are a participant in the collective of our lives we must begin to cultivate initiative and invitation in our relationships. If we are a facilitator we must begin to cultivate interactive dialogue, open systems and trusting relationships. If we are devoid of the collective in our lives, if we have no community; we must begin to move towards community. We must ask ourselves, when we have separated from community, whether we can truly reach our identity, passion and purpose on our own.

The next step in this journey to missional community involves asking ourselves what we are committed to. How much does discovering our identity, passion and purpose within the context of community matter to the meaning and quality of life here on earth?

Picture yourself just past the end of your life. You have been invited to your own funeral as an unseen guest. You are seated in the front row. You are the first to arrive and the last to leave. You watch the preparations, you see all the people, you hear all the voices. Who will come and why? What will you see and hear? Will it be the words you hoped would define your life? Will meaning be spoken? Will passion and purpose be evident? Will people know you knew who you were? If not, then are you just living to die? The journey to identity, passion and purpose is about *coming to life*. It is about our meaning here on earth. When we answer this question we answer the question regarding how our lives will be defined.

Are you ready to take the next steps towards your journey to identity, passion and purpose and towards passing it on to others and to the next generation? It begins when we identify relationships in our present spheres of influence that we could be transparent and open with about who we are. It begins in our work, our home and our churches.

It began for me when I started to "share" myself with others. Not just my opinions or even feelings, but who I really am. I risked being rejected and found I was embraced further. People could find themselves in my honesty. Whether over coffee, in a school meeting, at work or even in church gatherings, with one or with many I found myself being more real and honest, the good and the bad, the happy and the sad. I didn't allow myself to hide behind platitudes and being "together" all the time. I shed my religious tones to find God in the real me. I talk about doubts, fears, and pain, hopes and dreams. I talk about what I know and don't know. I deeply wanted to be authentic and in being authentic it called out others.

In being more transparent I discovered there were others who found my transparency not only disarming but refreshing and inviting. They, too, began to feel the permission to be transparent. A culture started to form. First it was one, then a few and now a church community carrying one another in disarming and refreshing honesty. Our church community is made up of these smaller communities of people who *"do life"* together. They have found common ground in their honesty and in being human, while still reaching for a life changing God together. It has become a place to call home, to be real, and to be missional. This is the how community begins in us.

Your next step is just as mine was. Identify those relationships in your life with which you can begin to be real and authentic. Begin today to ask God for His eyes to see where he has placed you and who, in the spirit of friendship, he wants you to journey alongside. You may begin to do that in your church, your work or your home. As you begin to "share" yourself you will find those who are ready to do the same no matter where they are in their spiritual journey. God will show you who they are as they will emerge in your life. Whether two or twenty, begin to gather together those that are ready and start this journey. If you are a leader in a community, let it begin with you. That is how missional community was formed in my life. The invitation to missional community awaits us all. The invitation to self-disclosure, to transparency and openness in relationship with God and others is available to us all. When we say "yes" to that invitation the journey through our brokenness to identity, passion and purpose changes us forever and provides a legacy for the next generation.

Chapter 8
Process Questions

1. Have you ever allowed yourself to be connected to the "first community" to receive the love and wholeness you need to start this journey? If not why?

2. How has individualism affected you, your habits and your relationships?

3a. Have you allowed yourself to be vulnerable and accountable in "community"? If not why?

3b. If no, what are you going to do about it?

4. How might not allowing "community" closer to you affect your discovery of your identity, passion and purpose?

5. How would you define your passion and purpose at this stage of your life?

6. What do you hope to be said about you at your funeral? Write it out for yourself.

For more information on growing missional communities see www.kelownavineyard.com or www.vineyard.ca. For other recources by Todd Rutkowski, see www.toddrutkowski.com.

FOOTNOTES

Chapter 1

1 Psalm 145: 4,5, New Living Translation

2 David Cohen, The Circle of Life (New York; Harper Collins Publisher, 1991), 66

3 David Cohen, The Circle of Life (New York; Harper Collins Publisher, 1991), 66

4 New Living Translation

5 Bill Carmichael, Seven Habits of a Healthy Home, (VMI Publishers, Sisters, Oregon, 2003); pg 183

6 Bob Boston, Kingdom Kids Resource manual, Langley Vineyard Church

7 John Wimber is the founder of the Association of Vineyard Churches

8 The Quest for the Radical Middle, Bill Jackson (Cape Town, Vineyard International Publishing, 1999), 45

9 Larry Crabb, Connecting (Nashville: WORD PUBLISHING, 1997), 51.

10 Larry Crabb, Connecting (Nashville: WORD PUBLISHING, 1997), 44

11 Larry Crabb, Connecting (Nashville: WORD PUBLISHING, 1997), 54

12 Author unknown

Chapter 2

13 The gospel of John 11: 1-37, New International Version

14 The gospel of John 11:3, New International Version

15 The gospel of John 11:21, New International Version

16 www.fatherforlife.org/divorce/dvrcrate.htm

17 Madeleine L'Engle, Walking on Water: Reflections of Faith and Art (New York: North Point Press, 1997), 68

18 Madeleine L'Engle, Walking on Water: Reflections of Faith and Art (New York: North Point Press, 1997), 111

19 Madeleine L'Engle, Walking on Water: Reflections of Faith and Art (New York: North Point Press, 1997), 46

20 Madeleine L'Engle, Walking on Water: Reflections of Faith and Art (New York: North Point Press, 1997), 114

21 Author unknown

22 Alfred H. Ells, Family Love – (Said by S.G. Goodrich, Thomas Nelson publishers, Nashville, 1991),

23 The Ten Unchangeables, Bill Gaither

24 Ephesians 3: 17-19, New Living Translation

25 The gospel of Matthew 3:17, New Living Translation

26 Bill Carmichael, Seven habits of a Healthy Home (VMI Publishers, Sisters, Oregon, 2003)

27 Sue Monk Kidd, The Story Shaped Life, Weavings (Jan./Feb.1989): p. 21

28 Bill Carmichael, Seven Habits of a Healthy Home, (VMI Publishers, Sisters, Oregon, 2003), p. 207

Chapter 3

29 The gospel of Luke 18:18-23 New International version

30 Valerie Bell, Getting out of your Kids Faces and into their Hearts, (Zondervan Publishing House, Grand Rapids, 1994), 72

31 The book of Proverbs 4:23, New International version

32 Real Moments, Barbara DeAngelis (Dell Trade Paperbacks, 1994) 212

33 Jeremiah 17:9, New International Version

34 The Gospel of Matthew 16:25, New International Version

35 Colossians 3:23, New International Version

36 The Gospel of John 8:7, New Living Translation

37 Note: While this story is true, some of the doctors history and exact locations within Angola are speculation.

38 The Book of Proverbs 4:23, paraphrased

39 Soul Survivor, Philip Yancey (New York, Doubleday, 2001) 293, 294

40 Soul Survivor, Philip Yancey (New York, Doubleday, 2001) 294

41 Soul Survivor, Philip Yancey (New York, Doubleday, 2001) 295,296

42 Soul Survivor, Philip Yancey (New York, Doubleday, 2001) 296, 297

43 Soul Survivor, Philip Yancey (New York, Doubleday, 2001) 296, 297

Chapter 4

44 The Book of Jeremiah 18:2-6, New International Version

45 The gospel of Mark 1:15, New Living Translation

46 The Book of Genesis 32:30, New International Version

47 The Book of Joshua 5:14, New International Version

48 The Book of Hebrews 12:5, New International Version

49 The Gospel of Matthew 20:21

50 The Gospel of John 9:53,54

51 Nancie Carmichael, Praying for Rain, Surrender & Triumph in Life's Desert Places; (Thomas Nelson, Nashville, 2001) p. 188

52 Paul Tournier, *Creative Suffering* (out of print)

53 The Gospel of Matthew 3:17, New International Version

54 The Book of Romans 8:26

55 The Book of Job 23:10, New International Version

56 Psalm 107:35-57, New King James Version

Chapter 5

57 Martin Luther King Jr., Strength to Love (Philadelphia: Fortress Press, 1981), 87

58 The Book of Hebrews 11: 32-39, New International Version

59 The Book of Hebrews 11:38, New International Version

60 Martin Luther King Jr., Strength to Love (Philadelphia: Fortress Press, 1981), 88

61 The Book of Romans 15:19-25, New International Version

62 The Book of Romans 1:10,11, New International Version

63 Martin Luther King Jr., Strength to Love (Philadelphia: Fortress Press, 1981), 92

64 Martin Luther King Jr., Strength to Love (Philadelphia: Fortress Press, 1981), 88

65 Philip Yancey, Disappointment with God (New York: Harper Paperbacks, 1988), 71

66 Philip Yancey, Disappointment with God (New York: Harper Paperbacks, 1988), 62,71

67 Philip Yancey, Disappointment with God (New York: Harper Paperbacks, 1988), 71

68 Philip Yancey, Disappointment with God (New York: Harper Paperbacks, 1988), 135

69 Martin Luther King Jr., Strength to Love (Philadelphia: Fortress Press, 1981), 88

70 Hebrews 12: 15, New King James Version

71 Martin Luther King Jr., Strength to Love (Philadelphia: Fortress Press, 1981), 89

72 Martin Luther King Jr., Strength to Love (Philadelphia: Fortress Press, 1981), 90,91

73 Martin Luther King Jr., Strength to Love (Philadelphia: Fortress Press, 1981), 91

74 Martin Luther King Jr., Strength to Love (Philadelphia: Fortress Press, 1981), 92

75 The Book of Acts 21:11, New Living Translation

76 The Book of Acts 21:13, New Living Translation

77 Martin Luther King Jr., Strength to Love (Philadelphia: Fortress Press, 1981), 96

Chapter 6

78 The Book of Ephesians 1:5, New International Version

79 Eugene Peterson, Leap over A Wall (San Francisco: HarperCollins, 1997), 17

80 I Samuel 15:11, New Living Translation

81 I Samuel 16:7, New Living Translation

82 I Samuel 16:11, New Living Translation

83 I Samuel 16:11, New Living Translation

84 Eugene Peterson, Leap over A Wall (San Francisco: HarperCollins, 1997), 17

85 I Samuel 16:12, New Living Translation

86 Eugene Peterson, Leap over A Wall (San Francisco: HarperCollins, 1997), 3

87 Eugene Peterson, Leap over A Wall (San Francisco: HarperCollins, 1997), 5

88 Eugene Peterson, Leap over A Wall (San Francisco: HarperCollins, 1997), 6

89 The Book of Acts 13:22, New Living Translation

90 Psalm 78:72, New International Version

91 The Gospel of John 13:3-5

92 I Samuel 17:33-37, New Living Translation

[93] I Samuel 17:26, New Living Translation

[94] T.H. White, The Sword and the Stone (New York: Philomel Books, 1965), 237- 240

[95] Jean Vanier, Community and Growth (New York: Paulist Press, 1998), 14

Chapter 7

[96] The gospel of Matthew 21:44, New International Version

Chapter 8

[97] I John 4:18, New Living Translation

[98] Dr. Henry Cloud & Dr. John Townsend, How People Grow (Grand Rapids, Michigan, Zondervan, 2001),126, 135, 136

[99] The gospel of Matthew 4- 18-21

[100] M. Scott Peck, The Different Drum (New York: Simon & Schuster, 1987), 88

[101] M. Scott Peck, The Different Drum (New York: Simon & Schuster, 1987), 89

[102] M. Scott Peck, The Different Drum (New York: Simon & Schuster, 1987), 89

[103] M. Scott Peck, The Different Drum (New York: Simon & Schuster, 1987), 89, 91

[104] Luke 9:46, New International Version

[105] M. Scott Peck, The Different Drum (New York: Simon & Schuster, 1987), 95

[106] The gospel of Matthew 26:33

[107] The gospel of Matthew 26:35, New International Version

[108] Gene Edwards, The Revolution, (Maine: Christian Books), 22

[109] Gene Edwards, The Revolution, (Maine: Christian Books) 22,23

[110] The Book of Acts 2:14-18, New Living Translation

[111] Gene Edwards, Revolution (Maine: Christian Books), 20, 21

[112] I Peter 2:9, New Living Translation

[113] Eugene H. Peterson, Leap Over A Wall (New York, HarperSanFransico, 1997), 20

[114] Eugene H. Peterson, Leap Over A Wall (New York, HarperSanFransico,1997), 19

[115] Jean Vanier, Community and Growth (New Jersey: Pauline Press, 1989), 86

[116] John 15:13, New Living Translation

[117] Darrell L. Guder, Missional Church, (Grand Rapids, Eerdmans Publishing, 1998), 81,82

[118] John 5:17, New Living Translation

IN MEMORY OF
Wally August Rutkowski
August 5th, 1939–December 26th, 1978

At the age of twenty, his linage was made known to him, though the time had not yet come for his revealing. With these words Elona challenged him: "rise above the height of all your fathers since the days of Glendill or fall into the darkness with all that is left of your kin."* For his father, Isildur had been overcome by evil and the question remained: Would Aragorn conquer the weakness of his bloodline and prevail over the darkness?

*Taken from
THE LORD OF THE RINGS